How to Get a Job in Japan

Get Hired and Get Here

by Andy Fossett

© 2010

TABLE OF CONTENTS

INTRODUCTION 4

MAJOR EMPLOYMENT OPTIONS 10

THINKING LONG-TERM 18

A NOTE ON AGE 21

SHADY BUSINESS 23

APPLYING FROM ABROAD 25

APPLYING FOR JET 29

APPLYING FROM JAPAN 37

HOP AND SHOP 40

CURRENT HOT SPOTS 42

TIMING YOUR JOB SEARCH 44

UNIVERSITY POSITIONS 48

IT AND TECHNICAL JOBS 51

OTHER OPTIONS 53

DUE DILIGENCE 56

ADVANCED QUALIFICATIONS 60

SEARCHING FOR JOBS ONLINE 65

FIRST CONTACT 71

RESUMES AND COVER LETTERS 72

YOUR PHOTO 79

REFERENCE LETTERS 82

INTERVIEWING 87

YOUR CONTRACT 92

YOUR VISA 97

START-UP COSTS 103

STUFF TO DO BEFORE YOU LEAVE 108

WHAT TO BRING WITH, WHAT TO LEAVE BEHIND 111

FIRST STEPS ON ARRIVAL 114

YOUR GAIJIN CARD 116

WORKING FOR A JAPANESE COMPANY 118

Tips from a Recruiter 126

RESOURCES 136

OUTRODUCTION 142

INTRODUCTION

A Short and Probably Superficial History of Work for Foreigners in Japan

Back in the day, I've heard that any English speaker could book a flight to Narita Airport near Tokyo and find a high-paying job in Japan within a week of landing. I know a few people that originally moved to Japan during those Golden Years, and they tell me it was truly a wondrous time.

Even when I took my first couple of visits here in the 90s, it was great to be a foreigner in Japan (despite the fact that there was still just one Starbucks in Shinjuku). Even in Tokyo, people went out of their way to be nice to me. I felt like a celebrity wherever I went. Families invited me to stay at their homes within minutes of meeting me. I got a lot of dates.

Then, sometime during the GW Bush Administration, things began to change for people looking to move to Japan.

For one thing, there were a lot more of us. I don't have any statistics handy, but when I finally moved here in 2003, there were other foreigners everywhere I went in Tokyo. And Starbucks too. There were places in smaller cities where non-Japanese were still few and far between, but you could no longer count on celebrity status by virtue of your birth.

Another change was that many Japanese towns and cities were in financial trouble. The economic downturn that had hit Japan hard at the end of the 90s didn't seem to effect the public sector very much at first, but when it came, it came down hard. Many towns went bankrupt and had to negotiate to be annexed by neighboring cities. These cities were often a lot tighter about budgeting and didn't like the idea of paying 36 million yen a year to entry-level teachers with no skills. Private dispatch companies began to thrive.

Meanwhile, the English conversation industry was booming. Anyone and everyone who grew up speaking English was getting hired by companies like NOVA to teach ineffective lessons to Japanese students who paid exorbitant prices on long-term contracts. It sounds like a recipe for success in the short run, but eventually, people began to see what a shifty system it was, and NOVA shifted right into bankruptcy in 2007.

Right when I was looking to return to Japan after a few months back in the States, the market was flooded with thousands of newly laid-off ex-NOVA employees willing to work for peanuts until they could afford airfare back home. Let me just say, it was a challenging job market to be competing in.

There are other large conversation schools still around, but they're extremely wary of becoming the next NOVA. I can't say I blame them.

To make a long story a little less convoluted, it's a lot more difficult to find a good job in Japan now than it was 15 years ago. Hell, even five years ago. There is more competition, starting salaries are lower, and being foreign is just not all that special anymore.

So how can you improve your chances?

Simple: you have to have a plan.

Know What You're Getting Into

Notice that nowhere above did I write that there are fewer jobs for non-Japanese in Japan. If anything, there are more. A lot more.

From 2010, English will be a compulsory subject for elementary fifth and sixth graders. Conversation schools have learned from NOVA's example and are adding more targeted services and with more flexible contracts. They're also being a little more selective with their hiring.

Thanks to the global economic uncertainty and the incredible rise of some of Japan's Asian neighbors, Japanese businesses are placing a premium on language skills. Television programs often feature visits to Chinese and Korean schools full of young children speaking English at a much higher level than their Japanese counterparts. This is a country that prides itself on its business savvy (whether or not you think that pride is well-deserved is another story), and they do not want to lose to Korea.

Also, you may not have noticed, but we've got this thing called the internet now. Yes, I know it's been around a while, but for much of the world, it's a new development, and most Japanese are still getting used to it. The cool thing about the internet is that it's turning English into the de facto lingua franca of the twenty-first century (wow, two Latin phrases in one sentence). Japanese people, especially younger ones, want to learn English so they can communicate online and learn about what's going on in places they find more exciting than where they are.

Speaking of excitement, tons of Japanese are really into travel, especially young women. At times it feels like more than half of the English learners I meet in Japan are young women who want to travel to Hawaii and New Zealand. There is a huge demand for people to teach English conversation without all the formal rules everybody hates learning in junior high school.

I Don't Want to Teach English

Not everyone is an aspiring edutainment pro. The world is full of different kinds of people who have different talents and skills and likes and dislikes. Unfortunately, most Japanese people have the image that all non-Japanese people are white Americans who exist for the sole purpose of teaching English. It isn't correct, and it isn't fair, but it's why the vast majority of non-Asian foreign residents of Japan are English teachers. It's an easy job to get.

I want to be clear about this at the beginning. This Guide is not specifically limited to teaching jobs, but much of the information and most examples will be related to that field. Even if you aren't interested in teaching long-term, I recommend trying it out, either as a gateway to something else, or as a source of supplemental income. Japanese people will probably assume that you are an English teacher anyway, so you may as well profit from it.

Still, I understand that many readers have higher aspirations for their futures than to be a foreign language teacher. I know I do. The good news is that there are a variety of jobs available here. The not-as-good news is that they are more difficult to find than the ubiquitous teaching jobs.

Not to worry. This Guide still has you covered. The principles and tactics behind the examples given will prove very effective in almost any field in Japan.

Which is the real value of this Guide anyway. Getting a job in Japan is different from finding employment in your home town. Besides the difficulties associated with international communication, relocation, etc., you also have to deal with Japanese people and their culture (and their stereotypes of *your* culture).

If parts of the Guide seem too focussed on English teaching to be of much help to you, take a step back and look for the underlying principles. I promise you'll find them just as relevant to whatever you are hoping to accomplish.

Your Battle Plan

So yeah, there are jobs. I promise you, there are jobs. But don't forget that there's also a lot of competition. To get a good job here, you really must have a plan, and that's what this book is about: crafting your battle plan for attacking the Japanese job market.

I'm going to go ahead and tell you the bad news first, because it may save you some time if you can't deal with it. The bad news is: you will probably not be able to find your dream job in Japan if you haven't already spent some time here.

I'm not telling you that it's impossible, but you can't expect to apply from overseas with no experience and no Japanese ability and get offered a great job with great pay and benefits in an area you want to live in. You can't expect that kind of deal at home, so you'd be silly to expect it another country, right? I knew you'd agree. Which is why I know you want to come up with the best possible plan to get yourself over here so you can start looking for the job you really want.

There. I said it.

This Guide is about strategy, so I'm going to go ahead and give away a key strategy for finding a great job in Japan:

Find a not-so-great job first.

Find a job that you can do, one that isn't bad, but maybe isn't where you want to stay for several years - a stepping stone job.

Take that job and get over here. Fulfill your contract, all the while building your knowledge and experience and shopping the job market from the inside. Then, make your move to find the job you really want.

Or, you just may get lucky and hit a home run on your first attempt.

In either event, this guide will make sure that you are adequately prepared with a solid strategy that will see you through to your ideal conditions. No matter where you are now or what skills you have, you can put together a plan that will get you where you want to be: teaching English, bartending, practicing Zen Buddhism, IT ... whatever.

Please Read Everything

You may find chapters or sections that you think don't apply to you. And they may not - *yet*. Still, the more knowledge you have, the better prepared you will be to take advantage of opportunities that lead in the direction of your dream job.

I encourage you to read this entire Guide, *especially* the parts that don't seem to be related to how you see yourself in the future. Doing so will provide you with a wider network of association and techniques (remember what I wrote about principles and tactics above) that will prove valuable to you at some point in your stay in Japan.

When you do find your first Japanese job and begin living here, I encourage you to read this Guide again and see what can be applied to your new situation. There's a very good chance that your new perspective will give you even more ideas of how to apply the information included here.

With Preparation, Anything is Possible

Times have changed, and it's no longer easy to just show up and begin living the good life right away, but don't let anyone tell you it isn't possible to live a totally fulfilling life doing things you truly love in Japan. It is possible, and with the right preparation, it's inevitable.

This Guide will prepare you to find the best possible work so you can live your dreams in Japan.

MAJOR EMPLOYMENT OPTIONS

There are a lot of different things one can do for a living in Japan. You could be a professional juggler, provided you can produce legitimate contracts and a convincing work history to immigration. There are also a good number of technical and research opportunities for those who have the necessary experience their particular fields.

However, if you are reading this, your best bet to find a job in Japan quickly and easily is probably going to be by teaching English. Of course, there are other languages - French is always in demand - but you're reading this in English, so I'm going to assume that it's your native tongue. In such a case, there are many positions available to you in the English teaching industry.

As an aspiring English teacher, there are four main roads to Japan. These are the classic entries through which more than 90% of all westerners initially make their livings in Japan. They are:

- JET Programme
- Dispatch company ALT
- Big conversation school
- Mom and pop conversation school

In the first two, you'll work as an ALT, or assistant language teacher. In these positions, you work at public schools with a Japanese teacher. The second two options may call you various things, but you'll typically teach a mix of young children and older adults from a company curriculum. Let's look at each of these in detail.

JET Programme

JET stands for Japan Exchange and Teaching, and "Programme" is just a fancy way to write "program" that somebody in Tokyo probably thought made them look smart.

JET is great in many ways, but its naming already reveals a bit of the frustration that JET participants will likely deal with during their tenures. The Ministry of Education in Japan models its English curricula on North American English, as it is the variant of the language spoken most commonly and widely throughout the world. However, the program is named with the European spelling. It looks confused at best, and hypocritical at worst.

I have fond memories of JET, as that's how I first found work in Japan. Once I was accepted, the JET liaison at the consulate handled everything, and all I had to do was show up at a meeting a few days before departure to collect my visa and plane ticket.

On arrival at Narita too, everything was easy as could be. We grabbed our bags and were taken to our hotel for a few days of training. Then, we were all shipped off to various areas of the country, where we met our supervisors and were shown home. Easy, easy, easy.

My home was a furnished house with several rooms, two A/C units, a washer and dryer, and a car. All that for the low, low price of 60000 yen (then, about $550 US) each *year* in maintenance. The house was about five minutes from my school and right next to the city office, meaning my supervisor was never very far away if I needed anything. She set up my bank account and helped me get a mobile phone. She even came over after work to teach me how to use my Japanese appliances and show me where the nearest grocery store was.

The other good thing about JET is that the pay is above average for ALT positions. It also includes enrollment in national the health insurance and pension program. There is a built-in support network of other JETs in your area and a program coordinator at the prefectural office, with everyone working together to make life easy for each other. You'll be invited to lots of parties and basically have an easy ride for one to three years. Now, even up to five years.

JET probably sounds great right about now, but there are a few drawbacks. For one thing, you probably won't have any choice over the location of your placement. Most JET positions are in fairly rural locations or small, isolated cities. If you absolutely have to live in Tokyo, just forget about JET. You will have a chance to name a preference, but do not expect that this will be considered in any way. You will be placed in an area that needs a native English teacher, and your placement will likely appear totally random.

Concomitant with having all the difficult decisions made for you and plenty of help with anything even mildly important comes the price of not getting to do some things you may want to. Some people have very helpful and understanding supervisors who will go out of their ways to make everything easy and wonderful. Some JETs don't get so lucky. The unofficial JET motto is "every situation is different," and that means that some people might get a sweet deal like I did, and others may not.

You could have to spend a year living in a run down apartment with no heater or A/C and an insect problem. I had a friend who lived in an old *koban*, or "police box." You may be required to bike to work, and it may be pretty far. You might have to report to the board of education office everyday for six weeks of sumer vacation and stare at the wall.

Even if you love it, you can only do JET for three years unless you are offered an extended contract to teach elementary school for up to five years. When I did JET, there were no extended contracts, so I had to leave my sweet, sweet life in the Japanese countryside after only three years.

Also, JET is selective. The exact figure changes every year, but on average, less than a third of applicants are accepted. The joke used to be that the other two-thirds ended up working for NOVA. However, don't take this to mean that JET is elite. There plenty of losers on JET. The majority of JETs are fresh college grads, many getting their first taste of life outside their home countries. Very few JETs have any teaching credentials of any sort, or even any real interest in teaching as a career.

JETs get their hands held by their local government offices, yet get paid extremely well. This can breed resentment from others. Add to that the fact that many JETs lack any semblance of professionalism, and you can see why they don't have the best reputation among other teachers (Japanese and foreign, alike). This isn't to say that JETs are really looked down on, but they aren't really considered real teachers or professionals by many people in the English education industry.

Dispatch Companies

A dispatch is a company that obtains large numbers of contracts from local boards of education and then hires teachers to fill those positions. Well-known dispatches are Interac, Altia Central, and Borderlink, abut there are many others. Though better-known as conversation schools, Geos and ECC also have dispatch divisions. Almost any company can form a dispatch division and bid on contracts, so there are many smaller dispatch agencies as well.

I'll go ahead and give you the bad news here. These companies are, without exception, profit driven. They are middlemen. They make their money off the labor of others. Certain of them are more or less evil than others and provide excellent training and support. However, all of them share the distinction of competing in a flooded market for broke clients.

The way it works it this: The dispatch companies approach the boards of education about providing teachers. This sounds like a good deal the boards, because taking care of foreigners is not easy. If some company can relieve them of that burden, they don't have to be responsible for it. However, funds are limited, so the boards usually hold a bid in which competing dispatch companies try to bid as low as they can while still fulfilling their contracts. They then pass these "savings" along to the ALTs in the form of low pay and few benefits.

It's not that the people working at dispatch companies are bad (not most of them, anyway). The problem is that the system is price-driven.

Criticism aside, I have worked for two different dispatch companies, and had reasonably good experiences with both. The downside is lower pay than JET and less support. You'll have a lot more things to figure out on your own if you come to Japan to work for a dispatch company. Still, you'll also have more freedom, and it's not like they're going to totally hang you out to dry. The majority of dispatch companies that hire overseas applicants will sponsor your visa and assist you with finding housing. They also tend to offer training and help with administrative issues.

See? Not necessarily bad guys after all.

Every company has a different standard contract, and you can get a good snapshot of their "package" by looking at the positions they offer online. Some companies offer slightly higher pay. Some have better benefits, like long summer holidays or subsidized apartments. Some companies tend to offer positions centered on a specific geographical area, while others are seemingly everywhere. You'll have to weigh all of these factors for yourself when you're deciding where to apply and what offers to consider.

English Conversation Giants

The English conversation Giants are huge corporations that offer the educational equivalent of fast food. These companies put up branch schools at every major train station and in any city they can find on a map. They are heavily advertised in print, on TV, and online. You can't ride a subway train without seeing at least five ads for English conversation schools. They are ubiquitous.

These schools sell contracts to students based on a certain number of lessons per week over a period of X months of study. They may have various courses for beginners or advanced students. Some specialize in teaching children. Some of them teach private "man to man" lessons. The flavors vary, but the system is always based on selling contracts to students. If you work at one, you'll probably be reminded of this daily.

There are some ups and downs to teaching English conversation. You'll get to interact with a wide variety of people. The pay is usually reasonable on an hour-by-hour basis. Many of the larger companies will help you with accommodation and can sponsor your visa. You'll have a built-in support network in your coworkers who can help show you around town and help you figure things out. Some companies offer freelance contracts with flexible holidays.

On the downside, you'll do most of your teaching during the afternoons and evenings. You'll probably teach fifty minutes out of each hour with only short breaks and find yourself eating most of your meals from a microwave. You'll almost certainly have to work on weekends, at least sometimes, and you may not get to choose your holidays at all if you can't find someone to cover your classes (remember that the company has to honor their contracts with the students…).

Most westerners living in Japan who didn't come here on JET end up working at an *eikaiwa* (the Japanese word for these schools) for at least a short while. Some people work there for years. It really depends on what suits your tastes. If you can handle working most nights and weekends and enjoy a busy atmosphere, you'll probably fit right in at any of the Giants. A few of them pay better than many dispatch agencies, so if you're willing to trade time off for extra cash, these schools could be the way to go.

English Conversation Schools

In this category, I'm including independent schools, small chains, and franchise schools. The daily operations are very similar to those above. You'll be teaching the same mix of kids, homemakers, and professionals. You'll use similar workbooks and teach in similar small rooms.

The difference is that each one of these smaller schools is an entity unto itself. The reason I list them separately is that you can't be certain what to expect form them. This isn't necessarily a bad thing - it's just that the conditions vary widely.

If you are considering a small conversation school, check them out and get a feel for what they expect from you as well as what they're offering. Know where you'll live and what the students are like. Ask a lot of questions. There are some sweet deals out there with great schools who are willing to take great care of the right person. But some places will try to rip you off. If you get a bad feeling about a school, or if they make unrealistic promises, I'd advise you to stay away. If they are friendly and open, there's a good chance you can work out a deal that benefits everyone.

Just remember that each position will be different. Do your homework and weigh the pros and cons before you sign any contracts.

Is that all?

Of course, there are other employment options in Japan besides teaching English. Even in the English teaching industry, there are plenty of other opportunities. There are business English schools that differ in several ways from the conversation schools. There are international schools. There are private daycares. There are human resources and administrative positions at dispatch companies. There are college teaching positions too. However, all of these are much fewer in variety and opportunity than the four main options above.

If you don't want to teach, or aren't a native English speaker, there are still options. I'll get into some of those in another chapter.

THINKING LONG-TERM

The One-Two Strategy

It's entirely possible that you will find a great job advertised that matches your qualifications and offers the kind of pay and benefits you feel you deserve. You can apply or such a position, score an interview, and get hired. It happens to lots of people every year.

But it may not work out just right. You may not find that perfect Goldilocks combination of work, pay, benefits, and location that you're searching for. In such a case, you may need to plan over a longer term. You'll need a strategy.

What follows is a strategy for getting a visa and getting to Japan legally and morally in a manner that allows you to build your resume so you'll be ready to take the perfect job when you find it from within Japan. Though the preceding sentence is more complicated than it needs to be, this plan does not have to be complicated at all. In fact, there are only two steps.

Step One - Get Over Here

Simple enough. Find a job in Japan that you can get. It might be at an *eikaiwa*, Westgate, or even as a volunteer (more on these options later). It doesn't matter.

If the positions you really want all seem to require qualifications you don't have, I suggest taking a job you are qualified for. It's not as romantic as following your dreams and trusting in the universe, but it gets results. Most of the non-Japanese I know in Japan live here because they wanted to live here. That sounds obvious, but the point is that they wanted to live here more than they cared what they were going to do once they did. Some of us got lucky, while others took crappy jobs at first.

If you don't get lucky, you might have to take a crappy job at first. You won't be the first one, and sometimes a job that looks crappy on paper can be great fun in person. I know several people that have worked in conversation schools (under conditions that make me squirm) for years and love it.

Don't knock it 'til you've tried it. Do your time in an entry level position, and the world will be your oyster. (Are there any other cliches I can use here?)

There are two major (and I mean really major) benefits you will get out of taking almost any job you are offered in Japan.

Visa
The most important thing you need to get from a potential employer is visa sponsorship. English conversation schools and programs like JET and Westgate will sponsor a visa for you. Once you get that work visa, you can continue to stay and work in Japan until it expires, and as long as you're working, you can extend the expiry of your visa.

If you have a visa, you'll increase your employment options dramatically. In many cases, this is worth a three or six month commitment at a job you don't really care much about.

Experience
Experience is another major benefit. Anything you do in Japan give you experience working in Japan. Teaching at a preschool can help you get a job teaching business English if you also have some professional experience. Take whatever experience you can get and leverage that towards where you really want to be.

Help Getting Established
Working in many entry-level programs also has benefits you may not have considered. Since you are coming over green, most companies that hire for these positions will hold your hand a bit with getting set up in Japan. They might help also have teacher training and language classes. Perhaps the best thing you'll get is a network of people who are in a similar

situation to yours or who were a year or two ago. This can be priceless assistance when you're trying to get established in Japan.

Step Two - Find a Better Job

This should be the easy part now. You'll be in Japan, have experience, have learned some Japanese, and generally be adapted to life in Japan. At this point you'll be able to apply all of the strategies in this Guide to search for and land the job you really want.

While you are working in your first Japanese job, you should also be learning. Learn how to make yourself a better worker and job candidate. Network. Make friends. Learn the ropes. Build your interpersonal and communication skills with Japanese and non-Japanese alike.

If you do these things, you will have a very good chance of being offered better jobs down the road. It's not rocket science, but I'm often surprised to hear people giving up on moving to Japan because they can't find the perfect job right away. Most people don't find the perfect job on the first try even in their home countries.

Think ahead. Plan ahead. Then start at step one. Eventually, you will get where you want to be.

A NOTE ON AGE

In the past, moving to Japan (especially to teach English) was an option apparently reserved for recent college graduates. In general principle, many employers in Japan do actively recruit candidates under the age of 35. There are several reasons for this, primarily based on the assumption years ago that the best situation for Japan would be to invite foreigners over to teach what they knew, and then thank them and send them on their ways after a couple of years.

It didn't quite work out that way.

As more people began moving to Japan from all over the world, a lot of us decided that we kind of liked it here. We discovered that learning to communicate in Japanese *wasn't impossible* after all, and that it made our lives here more interesting and comfortable than they would have been otherwise. We learned how to negotiate daily life and managed to find some level of acceptance among our Japanese peers (though we still are very rarely accepted by our Japanese counterparts as *true* peers).

To make a long story short, people are staying in Japan for longer now. To be sure, the majority of foreign residents *does* return home within two to five years, but the foreign-born population is slowly increasing. As a result, there are more and more of us here over the age of 30, and we're still managing to find somewhat meaningful work.

Of course, the older you get, the more factors you have to consider when moving to another country. Will your work experience be as highly sought after in a new environment? Will you adapt easily to a new culture? If you have a family, there are even more factors to think about.

The fact is that you don't have to be 22 years old to find work in Japan. Many companies respect the experience and stability they see "grown-up" candidates as representing. People over 30 are, on the whole, less likely to engage in the kinds of rowdy and disrespectful behavior that many Japanese associate with non-Japanese youth.

Youth can still be a commodity. Some employers will not hire candidates over a certain age (and discrimination based on sex and age, legal or not, are widely practiced in Japan). As many of the positions available to foreigners are essentially entry-level, older candidates may find that their Japanese coworkers have a hard time understanding their motivation to "start over." Still other employers might find it awkward to supervise someone who is senior to them.

The point is, it could go either way, and you'll have to check up on the particular industry or position to know for sure. One thing worth noting is that older candidates with good Japanese skills have very good chances of landing work in professional or teaching fields. It really comes down to the specific employer and position under consideration.

As with all things, age can be an asset or a curse, depending on how you frame it. Don't be discouraged if you're not as young as you once were (I think that's all of us...). If you do your research and communicate your benefits to potential employers skillfully, you should have no problems finding employment anywhere in the world. Even in Japan.

SHADY BUSINESS

When I set out to write this guide, my goal was to make it the most complete source of information on finding employment in Japan available. That said, there are a few things I have left out.

Every now and again, I run across a website or a forum post in which somebody claims to have moved to Japan without going through certain necessary steps. Sometimes, I hear stories about people living in Japan for extended periods on a tourist visa and taking weekend trips to Korea every three months to renew it. I once had a friend who worked illegally at a pachinko machine factory with no visa (and I did a stint picking green tea).

Japanese immigration is getting tougher all the time, and there's no guarantee that you can get away with "unorthodox" tactics to move here.

There are many immoral and marginally-legal things one could do to move to Japan too, and some of them are pretty easy to pull off. I've known a few "visa bandits" who agreed to work for one company to get visa sponsorship, just to back out of their contracts before the first day of work and look for another job. All this kind of thing accomplishes is making companies hesitant to hire from overseas and sponsor visas.

I won't be telling you how to do any of these things primarily because they are shady. They also make the job market even tougher on honest people like you and me. This Guide is about strategy, but it isn't about lying or cheating to get ahead.

This is not a guide to tricking the Japanese government and scamming your employers.

Your best bet is to go through the proper channels and do things right the first time. It may seem like a pain in the ass to begin with, but I can virtually promise you that you will save time and money by just going ahead and playing the game.

As satisfying as it may feel to try to outsmart everyone else who has come here to work, the smartest people I've met in Japan are the ones who have learned to navigate the system well enough to live comfortably and easily. There are plenty of legitimate opportunities here, so please don't make things hard on others by doing something stupid.

The strategies in this Guide are by far the surest, most-proven methods available to find employment and get yourself to Japan legally and comfortably.

APPLYING FROM ABROAD

This is the category into which most people likely to read this book are going to fall.

I'll be honest with you at the outset - what you're trying to do is not easy. Lots of people have done what you're planning, and a good number of them fulfill their missions and either "go native" or return home after a period of time totally satisfied by their Japan experiences. An even greater number end up not able to find suitable employment (remember, it's not that it isn't available - you have to *find* it) or end up moving here only to realize that Japan is not for them.

All of this is just to say that, unless you have already lived in Japan, you are going to have many challenges waiting for you here - many positive, and some not so nice. The first of those challenges is connecting with potential employers from across an ocean. This does not have to be unpleasant, but it does require a little bit of work.

Basically, you need to go through seven phases to get from where you are now to working in Japan. I'll walk you through each step in detail later, but here's an overview of the process:

Research
You got lucky with this one, as almost everything you need to know is included in this guide. Still, you will want to look more deeply into specific companies and positions. I've included a ton of additional resources to check out in the Resources section (clever, I know).

Contact
After you have an idea of where you want to live and whom you'd like to work for, it's time to begin making contact. Increasingly, this will take the form of an email or online form, but there are still companies that list phone numbers for recruiting issues, and you should take advantage of the

opportunity to ask questions and get a feel for the company. That information will be a big asset to you in preparing your application materials.

Application

Once you get in touch with recruiters, company representatives, school owners, or whomever, you'll need to submit your application documents. Every position is going to have different requirements, so be sure to follow instructions, but you will probably need to provide a resume, references, and some sort of statement about what your goals are and why you are a good candidate.

Interview

If things go well, you'll be granted an interview. Some companies may ask you to interview in Japan. If this is possible for you, I won't recommend against it (it's a good excuse to visit Japan...), but I'd make sure you do your research first as this is an expensive interview. Make sure you really want to work for that company (it's very rare for a company in Japan to agree to cover your airfare for an interview).

Some large companies that hire a lot of foreign employees will make an annual recruiting trip to various countries, and these dates are often posted on their websites. Knowing the interview schedule is a necessity when applying to these companies as you may only have one chance to catch their interviewers near where you live.

A few companies even have offices in countries where they do a lot of recruiting. I know that two of the major English conversation chains have offices in the US. These companies recruit year-round, and it may be worthwhile to travel to their offices for an interview.

Contract

After you interview, you'll be notified within a few days whether or not you are going to be offered a position. In some cases, details may be available, but sometimes, the specifics are not forthcoming. In any case, get all the information you can and start preparing to move.

You will be given a contract. This is very serious business, so please look it over closely and ask questions about anything that differs from what you had expected or discussed in the interview. Most contracts are built from a template, so it's possible that errors were made. Address these now.

Visa Acquisition
As you know, you will need a visa to work in Japan. If you're applying form overseas, you'll probably have your employer handle most of the details for you after you sign your contract. In most cases, the process takes a couple of months and will require you to make a trip to the nearest Japanese consular office or embassy.

Moving
Finally, you have to get your life all boxed up and moved to Japan. This includes physical articles as well as legal and emotional issues. Then you'll get the keys to your new home and begin to unpack. While this Guide is mostly focused on finding employment, there is also some advice on moving and getting yourself established once you touch down in Japan.

Step by Step

Getting through all seven phases takes time and patience, but it doesn't have to be overwhelming. Just take it one step at a time and follow the strategy as outlined in the following chapters.

Remember that you are combining two major life changes here: making a career change and moving to a new country. This is not simple, and you are bound to experience frustration at various points along the way. This is not impossible, and by reading this guide, you have a huge advantage in terms of information and experience to lead you in the right direction.

Even if you begin to get confused, or feel that your questions are going unanswered, read to the end of the guide, and you will probably find the gaps being filled in gradually as you go along.

APPLYING FOR JET

If you've looked into teaching English in Japan at all, chances are you have heard of the JET Programme. It's definitely the most well-known path to teaching in actual Japanese schools, and it has the potential to be a really sweet deal for certain types of people.

I've already discussed the basics of what the program is and what it entails. For a more complete picture, you can get the official details from the website listed in the Resources section.

JET Positions

I should also mention here that there are JET positions besides ALT. In fact, there are two. One is the SEA - Sports Exchange Advisor. I've never met or heard of an SEA, though I'm sure they exist. If you are an exceptional athlete and have an interest in Japan, you should get in touch with your nearest Japanese consulate for details and requirements.

The other JET position is called CIR - Coordinator for International Relations. This is a non-teaching position that is usually based in the prefectural office. It's an executive level job, though the pay is the same as the ALT position. As it requires working in a Japanese office environment, the CIR position is usually recommended for those with exceptional Japanese language skills (a third language is also an advantage) and knowledge of Japanese culture. If this is your first experience with Japan, CIR probably isn't for you.

The huge majority of people interested in JET are going to be applying for the ALT position, so that's what we'll focus on in this chapter.

Your Odds

As JET is the most well-known program, it's also the most applied-for. JET spots pay well and are usually easy. There is a lot of competition. The year that I applied, we were told in Tokyo orientation that less than 30% of all applicants to the program had actually been hired. The year that I served as a JET interviewer, we only passed one candidate out of nine from my group.

Overall, JET places roughly 5,000 ALTs. About half of those re-contract each year, which leaves between 2,000 and 3,000 available positions in any given application period. About half of these are recruited from the US, though nearly 40 countries are represented.

The number of new jobs available each year depends on the number of JETs who choose to end their contracts and leave the program. Apparently, this number has been declining in recent years. This means that there are fewer jobs and probably even more competition as the industry gets more saturated and competitive from the Japan side.

Don't let this scare you off. You want the process to be competitive, because that narrows the field to those candidates that have the most to offer (by which I mean **you**).

Overview of the Process

Going to Japan with JET can be a great experience in several ways. For one thing, they take all the confusion and work out of the "getting there" part of the experience. Should you be accepted, you basically just let the consular office handle your entire visa, immigration, and travel situation. In fact, you have no choice in the matter. Until you are shipped off to your new home and given the keys to your apartment after training, you will essentially just be following directions in a herd of other newbies.

The application process for JET is actually pretty straightforward. You have to fill out an application, write an essay, get references, show that you have graduated from college (or will before departure), and prove your nationality. This is all due during December of the year prior to your eventual departure (which will be in late July or early August). Then, you wait for a few months.

If your application is accepted, you'll hear in either February or March when you need to show up for your interview. If you live in a city with a consulate, this is no big deal, but otherwise, you'll have to make plans to travel at your own expense to the consulate at the appointed time. After the interview, you'll return home and, again, wait for a few months.

You should be hearing something during May if you're hired. You'll be notified of either a placement or an alternate placement. If you don't get word as soon as you'd like, keep waiting. Some applicants don't get official placements until as late as the end of June. This is because the local boards of education (who are your actual employer while on JET) tend to drag their feet about making decisions (any decision at all, really). If the BOEs that are considering your application slack, you may find yourself getting very anxious as July approaches.

In many cases, you will receive a letter from your predecessor who will be leaving your job about a week before you show up (and if you're lucky, will leave some beers in the fridge for you). I got a letter from my predecessor about two weeks before I received word from the consulate. This letter should give you some details about where you'll be living and working if you accept your assignment.

Some people don't accept (usually when they find out that their placement is nowhere near Tokyo and their town has a population of less than 10,000. If this happens to you, don't freak out - I promise it will be better than you expect), and their placements are then offered to alternates. This process again takes time. Alternates can expect a lot of waiting and uncertainty.

Once you are offered a position and accept the assignment, you will have to fill out a medical questionnaire and get a doctor to certify that you are "healthy." This is typical in Japan, as all employers are responsible for making sure their full-time employees are covered by health insurance. On JET, you'll be signed up for the national health and pension plan.

After you prove your health, you wait a little longer, after which you'll have a pre-departure orientation - usually a day or two before departure.

Then, before you know it, you'll be landing at Narita, and things will speed up considerably.

The Application

Though long and detailed, the actual application is easy enough to figure out. Just fill in the required information and gather the necessary materials.

Statement of Purpose
The part of the application most likely to cause you any loss of sleep is the Statement of Purpose. Despite that fancy name, it's really just an essay. When I interviewed candidates for JET, we were sent copies of the applications and essays to review before the interview date. Since the application information is rather dry, the essays were the best material we had to try to get to know the candidates before meeting them face to face. Do not underestimate how powerful an impression your writing will make.

When you write your essay, I recommend reviewing the section on resumes and cover letters. Use your essay to highlight the strengths you focus on in your application. Bring out details and stories that illustrate why you're a great candidate and would be an asset to the program. You need to give your interviewers an idea of who you are. Show a little personality, so they can imagine what your voice sounds like and what kinds of facial expressions you make. This can help you build near-instant rapport when you have your interview.

Another point to consider is proofreading. You want to remember that you are going to be representing "correct English" as a teacher. You cannot afford to have spelling and grammatical errors in your Statement of Purpose. Not only does it look unprofessional, but it casts doubts on your qualifications to teach. Proofread your essay several times. Print it out on real paper and show it to friends or a professor. You cannot be certain enough that your essay is perfect. Do not save this part for last because it is one of the most important parts of your application.

Also keep in mind that the typography requirements for the essay are rigid. Paper size, margins, font size, page numbering, etc. need to be followed exactly. If your essay is long, it will be truncated. When I was an interviewer, we had two candidates whose essays were incomplete - meaning they were cut off at two pages, and we didn't know how they were supposed to end. Can you guess what our initial impression of these candidates was?

Write about why you want to participate in JET and why you would be an asset to the program. Tell your interviewers why you are interested in Japan and what makes you think you are cut out for the ALT (or CIR) position. Write about international experiences where you've had to communicate with people from other cultures. Write about any teaching you've done, even just tutoring. Mention any professional experience that pertains to the position for which you're applying.

You should also mention your goals. Address how you think you'll benefit and grow as a person from experiencing JET and life in Japan. How do you plan to use your experience beyond JET? Can you turn your experience into an asset for your community or in an international arena? Think of your life ten years after JET and imagine how JET will have played into that image.

There are also a few things you should avoid mentioning in your essay. Anything that doesn't sound positive or supportive should be omitted. Do not criticize others or make assertions about politics or moral issues. Avoid making generalizations or assumptions about Japan - remember that every situation is different, and you are not an expert yet. Don't dwell on how much you love karate or haiku. Those interests are great, but they will not make up the bulk of your experience as a JET.

Generally, don't write about things that cast you in an unprofessional light or make you appear unstable or unhealthy. Try to keep your wording concise and to the point. Trying to appear "smart" by using big words and long sentences is a tactic guaranteed to backfire. Your interviewers are almost certainly more educated than you are and have much more experience with Japan, so attempting to impress them with your knowledge is probably a mistake. Discussion of what you want to learn will impress them much more than any mention of what you already know.

References
You'll need to provide two sealed reference letters with your application package. Refer to the section on reference letters for more detail. For JET, I also recommend showing your references copies of your Statement of Purpose so they can get an idea of who you want to present yourself.

The Interview

The same rules apply for the JET interview as do for any other. Be prepared and on time. Look your best. Have some questions ready to ask your interviewers. Smile.

Interviews for JET are always done by a panel consisting of a consulate staff member, someone from the academic or business community with ties to Japan, and a former JET.

All three are "real" interviewers in the sense that their questions count and they will discuss your application and interview performance as a group after you've left. I've read elsewhere that the consulate staff member is the only interviewer you need to impress, but this was definitely *not* my experience. In my group, we talked about the pros and cons of each candidate before coming to a consensus on our recommendations for that candidate's application, and the consulate staff were genuinely interested in the opinions of the other interviewers.

As a candidate, you want to show that you can interact with different types of people and communicate well while responding to a variety of questions. The multiple interviewers are there to challenge you, but also to increase your chances of connecting well enough to express your strengths and passions.

Speaking of passions, I know I've mentioned it before, but loving *anime* is not going to impress JET interviewers. Please do not confuse "Japanese culture" with things like *manga* in your interview or essay. Instead, tell us about what you love to do (as opposed to what you love to consume) and how you think that can be useful to your students and community in Japan. If an interviewer asks you a question that goes against an assumption you've made about Japanese life or people, don't argue. Take it as a chance to clarify your own knowledge and show that you can learn from others.

The interviewers really do genuinely want to find the best possible candidates. If you have good qualities and a real desire to share your culture, learn about Japan, and teach, your interviewers definitely want to recommend your application.

Wrap Up

That's about all there is to say about applying for JET. There are whole websites devoted to this process and countless blogs written by JETs and former JETs describing their interviews and experiences. You should definitely read up on them, but remember to take everything you see online with a grain of salt.

If things go well, you will (after some time passes) be notified and offered a placement. If you do come to Japan on JET, remember that ESID, every situation is different, and you'll be fine.

APPLYING FROM JAPAN

If you live in Japan already, you've got things pretty easy, and you know it. You also know that, despite your greatly expanded employment options, you're just another foreigner to most Japanese companies, and there's a lot of competition for the really good jobs.

If you don't live in Japan yet, still read this chapter. After you have been here for a while, you may find yourself interested in changing jobs (review the chapter on long-term strategy).

This is going to be a short chapter because you know most of what you need already (or will by the time you're ready to use this advice). I mostly want to call your attention to a few key facts and point to towards a couple of resources you may not have considered.

Key facts

- There are a ton of new jobs available teaching English in elementary schools. You can find these most often through recruiters and sometimes through municipal boards of education.
- Direct hire positions are getting fewer and farther between due to the economy and apparent benefits to BOEs of hiring dispatch companies to handle "the ALT problem" for them. Don't give up - such positions do exist, and you may be able to negotiate a new one if you really try.
- If you are applying for positions in public schools, emphasize any language skill you have (*usually* - some positions want to only speak English). Many preschools and children's programs don't want you to use Japanese at all, so you should not try to show how fluently you can speak with interviewers in such

cases. How do you know whether you should speak Japanese or not? Ask them.
- Now that you've been here for some time, you know people. Who you know is more important than what you know. Get references, get introductions, get your friends to spread the word that you are looking for work.
- A couple of part time jobs can equal or exceed the pay of a full time job in some cases. However, be sure to consider other benefits such as insurance, transportation reimbursement, and time spent commuting before you jump for a pay increase.

Resources you may not have considered

- City home pages and newsletters. Often there are job openings posted in the announcements section.
- Hello Work - This is the national employment program, and they most certainly do have jobs for English speakers and foreigners. There is Hello Work in all major cities. Just show up and ask them how to search the database. The good news is that most of these jobs do not get many applicants.
- Local or regional classifieds and info websites. There are a number of English sites devoted to providing local and regional information for foreigners, and many of them have classifieds. Guess what those ads are advertising. If you said "jobs," you are right on the money.
- Most cities have an international friendship association. Larger cities may even employ foreign residents for positions in international relations. Even if they don't have any jobs to offer, they can probably help you find something. You just need to get in touch and ask for help. That's what they're there for.

- Open up Google and type in the name of your city in kanji along with □ □ and □ □. Behold: teaching jobs not advertised in English.

None of these are top secret, but the number of people who know about and use them is definitely relatively minor. For example, you may see that a classified ad on *Kansai Time Out* has been viewed 100 times, but maybe only ten of those people applied - much better odds than Gaijin Pot...

Another thing you can use to your advantage is some Japanese conversation skill and a phone. Sounds crazy, I know, but you would be stunned by how few applicants bother call the phone numbers listed on local classifieds. It's almost guaranteed to at least land you an interview if you can call the number and express your interest in Japanese. Even if you can't speak much, try. They love it when you try.

This can work for boards of education too, though you'll need to have considerable speaking skill. Just call up the *gakko kyoiku* department in March and ask if they are hiring ALTs for the following year. I did this on a whim once and was invited to interview. I felt so lucky, I couldn't keep my mouth shut, and one of my friends ended up applying for the same position. He works there now.

Just don't forget that living in Japan gives you a lot more options. Take advantage of them. As the saying goes, the things that got you to this level will not take you to the next one. You will have to use different tools and tactics to get a better-than-entry-level job in Japan, but it can be done.

Use your knowledge, use your contacts, and use your communication skills to ask for introductions and interviews.

HOP AND SHOP

All in all, it's easiest to apply for a job in Japan from Japan. There are several benefits, such as the ability to make contact easily and interview in person at a mutually convenient time. The downsides are the cost of getting here and the unfortunate illegality of entering the country on a tourist visa with the intention of looking for work.

As to that last part, it's not really anything to worry about. When questioned at immigration, simply tell them the truth: you have come to learn more about Japan and get a feel for various aspects of its culture. If you come all this way, definitely take some time to see the sites and travel around a bit. Definitely *don't* come to Japan if you aren't interested in hanging out and learning a few things. If you manage to squeeze in a job interview or two, there shouldn't be anything wrong with that. Just don't mention it at border control.

Also note that, in order to get a tourist visa upon arrival in Japan, you'll need to have a return flight ticket. Japanese people are freaked out by the thought of illegal immigrants (mostly from the Philippines and Brazil), so your friendly border agent will want to have some assurance that you plan to eventually go home.

If you are planning to visit Japan and do a little job hunting on the side, there are a few things you should keep in mind.

- Japan is expensive. You will not be able to land at Narita, call up a recruiter, interview, and get hired in a span of less than a couple of weeks. Unless you'll be staying with friends or family, you may find your funds running very short.
- You'll need a phone. They are available for rental at the airport (see the above note about Japan being expensive). You need to keep in contact with people,

- and phone is the preferred method for setting up interviews.
- You'll need internet access. This will be useful for getting directions to interview locations and sending our resumes and such. There are some internet cafes around larger cities, but they aren't always easy to find. Most hostels will be hooked up with internet access for guests.
- Timing can be sensitive. Most jobs for which you apply will have a set start date. You'll need to have your visa arranged (typically from within your home country) by that time.
- You will not be able to work on a tourist visa. You may be able to find a few folks to pay you for English conversation practice, but not enough of them to support eating and staying here for very long.

All of which is just to say, hopping over and shopping for a job is not the most efficient method for most people. If you already have connections and a place to stay, it can work for you, but you'll still need to get a COE and apply for a visa in your home country.

This isn't to say don't come to Japan. If you have the time and money, I definitely recommend visiting. Schedule a few interviews during your trip if you can. It's just probably not the cheapest or easiest option for most people.

CURRENT HOT SPOTS

Most people who dream of moving to Japan have fantasies of living in Tokyo and eating sushi all day. While Tokyo is the most populous city in the world, it would not be accurate to think that most people in Japan live in Tokyo, or even places *like* Tokyo. By extension, let me assure you that Tokyo is not the best place to look for work in Japan.

There are in fact tons of jobs in Tokyo. The problem is that they are the most competitive jobs in the country. It's like in "New York, New York" - if you can make it there, you can make it anywhere. But let's think about making it someplace else for a few minutes.

There are lots of great jobs outside of Tokyo, and most of them will offer better pay, cheaper living, and at least as much fun and culture. If you're serious about working in Japan, I suggest you do some research on the following areas, because it's likely you can find a job in at least one of them.

Become familiar with the basic geography of Japan and you'll have a point of reference when you read classifieds. There are 47 prefectures and "designated cities" in Japan. These are essentially the same as provinces or states.

By far, the majority of positions for foreigners advertised over the past couple of years have been in the area stretching from Kanto down through Tokai to the Kansai region. Kanto is the area around Tokyo, including Chiba, Saitama, Gunma, Tochigi, Kanagawa, and a few other prefectures. There are more jobs available as you move down the pacific coast through Shizuoka and into Aichi and Gifu.

Most JET positions are in rural areas, and Hokkaido and Hyogo Prefectures seem to have a high turnover rate.

When you are looking at advertised positions, you'll need to have some way of checking out their locations. One of the best tools for this is Wikipedia. The level of detail varies, but the articles on most cities of any size and all of the prefectures include such details as population figures, train lines, and of course, maps. Some posts have external links to other resources.

Of course, Google also has a lot to offer - maybe too much. With broad searches, there are just too many hits to sort through. Try using Google's blog search to find blogs written by people living on those areas, and you may get more information than you expect. Even better, you can make contact with the blog author and have a personal contact in a particular city or town to help you decide if you really want to live there.

Depending on whom you believe, the second largest city in Japan is either Yokohama or Osaka. Yokohama, Kanagawa Prefecture, flows right into Tokyo. The region surrounding these two cities is called Kanto. Osaka is further to the West, in an area called Kansai that also includes Kyoto and Kobe.

Other cities you may have heard of are Nagoya in Aichi Prefecture, Sapporo in Hokkaido, Hiroshima in Hiroshima, and Kawasaki in Kanagawa.

I'm got going to get very specific with the characteristics of each region because you can find that information online as it becomes relevant. However, I do advise you to take note of cities that seem to have a lot of jobs available and learn a little about them before applying.

TIMING YOUR JOB SEARCH

In a perfect world, jobs would just pop up when we decided we wanted them. And I would always have beer and ice cream in the fridge.

In the real world, things tend to work in cycles. Fashion, the economy, and the job market all have ups and downs, with varying predictability. It stands to reason that, to have the best chances of finding quality employment, you need to be looking at times when the best jobs are available. Fortunately, there are two major hiring seasons in Japan, and they happen like clockwork each year.

The First Window of Opportunity

You may think that this is only of concern to those in the education industry. After all, those jobs revolve around yearly school schedules and have a predictable cycle. However, what you may not know is that almost everything in Japan runs on the same yearly cycle, from April to March. *Nenmatsu* in Japan means finishing, shifting things around, and starting again for just about every group and organization you can think of.

It's also the time that most yearly contracts begin, which means that it comes at the conclusion of the Japan's primary hiring season. Since most new positions will begin in April, recruiting activities start to get underway in January and February, and these are best times to be getting in touch with prospective employers. A lot of good positions open up in March too, but keep in mind that, unless you are already living in Japan with a proper work visa, one month simply won't be enough time to get the logistics in order to move.

If you're looking to move to Japan from another country, I suggest getting your passport and resume together by the end of January, at the latest. You'll have to pass initial screening and arrange an interview before you can be considered for most positions, and only after that can a company begin the process of obtaining a Certificate of Eligibility for you. Also keep in mind that, since this is the busiest hiring and administrative season of the year, official document processing times are at their longest during this period.

It's certainly in your best interest to get moving with your applications as early in the year as possible. The last time I applied for work in Japan from overseas, I actually got hired in November of the previous year to begin work in April. It definitely helped that I was able to visit Japan around that time to interview in person (the company I ended up working for didn't even send a rep to interview in the US that year), but beginning the process well in advance by making contact early ensured that I had all of my paperwork in order - a signed contract and a shiny new visa in my passport - in time to fly over early and shop for an apartment.

It's still very possible for things to come together in a shorter timeframe, but giving yourself some extra breathing room can be a huge asset in terms of your planning and peace of mind when moving abroad.

Even though it is the peak period for new beginnings in Japan, April may not be the best time to plan on moving over here without some experience. As written above, it can be very difficult to get paperwork taken care of on a tight deadline due to the high levels of overall activity in the government offices where your forms and applications must be processed.

As cruel as it may seem, companies can't afford to guarantee contracts to prospective employees that they aren't sure will be able to begin work on time. If you are offered a job to begin work at a school in April, but your Certificate of Eligibility doesn't get processed until the end of March, you're not going to be able to acquire a visa and make transportation arrangements in time enough to begin work. Depending on your industry, this can cost your employers and their clients big-time. To play it safe, a lot of companies prioritize domestic hires for contracts beginning in April.

Another problem with trying to apply for an April start from overseas is that many of these jobs won't even be listed until March. This happens because that's when old contracts come up for renewal. In many cases, local boards of education don't finalize contractual decisions until after the new school year has already begun (this can make life extremely frustrating if you are working with a dispatch company). In such cases, it's almost impossible to get hired and get your paperwork in order in such a short time.

The Second Window of Opportunity

If April is beginning to look bleak, don't worry. There is a secondary hiring season that happens towards the end of summer. There are two good things about this. Firstly, if you couldn't get a visa by April but had everything else in order, there's still a good chance you can get a position lined up to begin in September. There are fewer visa applications processed after the first of the year, so the speed of delivery increases. Secondly, rainy season will be over when you get here.

Late July is when most JET Programme teachers will arrive in Japan. Most of August will be summer holidays, so JETs begin teaching around September. This is also when you'll begin work if you are hired by a company that successfully underbid JET in a recent contract offering.

A lot of things can happen to new hires over their first few months in Japan too. Some companies make bad hiring choices and end up having to fire new employees who didn't work out after April. Some people accept positions and just never show up. People change their minds about living in Japan. In these cases, employers will be needing to fill those contracted positions ASAP.

Finding Work at Other Times

Of course, these are not the only two chances you have to get hired. They are just the biggest peak periods. There are lots of jobs in Japan, and someone is always hiring. You just have to find them. Most of the large English conversation schools hire year-round.

If you aren't able to get everything working in your favor by April or late summer, and you can't see yourself working for one of the *eikaiwa* Giants, keep your eyes open for smaller schools that are looking to hire privately. These independent schools don't necessarily work on the same yearly cycle as everyone else because they are smaller businesses and aren't tied to the academic calendar.

To make things even better, some of them can be extremely flexible and generous if they believe they've found a great candidate with a good personality. I've heard of a few people who were hired by such schools and taken really good care of, with free accommodation, generous holidays, good pay, and built-in family and friends in the staff. I have one friend who works for such a school in Hokkaido and spends most of his winter snowboarding during the day and teaching during the evening. He loves his life (and doesn't plan on leaving his job anytime soon, so don't even ask...).

The biggest thing to keep in mind here is that, whenever you are thinking about coming to Japan, you will have to leave plenty of time for planning and preparation. Knowing when jobs are likely to come up can help you have all your ducks in a row so you can take advantage of advertised positions as they come up. The more prepared you are, the more likely a company is to offer you a contract.

UNIVERSITY POSITIONS

The first thing I should mention is that there are two basic kinds of university jobs available. One is as a "real" teacher, and the other is as a short-term instructor. Both have their pros and cons.

If you like to wear tweed...

For those with academic credentials, it's entirely possible to score a job with a Japanese university. There are English teaching positions, teaching positions in other fields, and research positions. Landing these jobs is very similar to what the process would be like in your own country.

You'll need to have at least an MA, but a PhD is preferable. You absolutely must have some publications to your credit, and references (the "who you know" factor) can be absolute gold. Teaching experience is a big plus too. In Japan, it also helps a great deal if you are under 35 (and male). In America, we would say that last bit is discriminatory, but discrimination is OK in Japan, so, if you want a Uni job in Japan, you'll need to have the best qualifications you can.

One thing you should keep in mind as you consider the possibility of attaining a position teaching at a Japanese university is that foreign instructors, as a rule, are not hired on tenure tracks. In all but rare cases, you will be hired on a contract that places strict limits on how long you can stay and what, if any, kind of professional benefits you can hope to receive. Though you will be expected to put in at least as much work as your Japanese counterparts, you will very likely not see the same rewards.

For more information on university work in Japan, you owe it to yourself to visit David Aldwinckle's site (listed in the

Resources section), as he has much more experience with Japanese universities than I do.

University jobs are not usually listed on the mega job search sites, but you can find them sometimes. In fact, many of them are not listed in English at all. The Resources section lists job boards that post university openings as well as other teaching jobs, but your best bet for finding a genuine academic appointment is to use your research and institutional contacts to make inquiries about programs and fellowships abroad.

For non-professorial types...

If you haven't spent much time in the ivory tower, you can still get university teaching experience in Japan. Provided you have a degree and some teaching experience (any teaching experience can help), there's a chance you could be offered a position as an English instructor.

The main gateway to this opportunity is a company called Westgate that places instructors in Japanese universities on a semester-by-semester basis. Westgate likes you to have teaching experience, since you'll be responsible to teaching several classes on your own. They can be a great way to get teaching experience, and they sponsor work visas.

Of course, it's not all peaches. The hours are typically quite long. You'll have to teach several classes a day and participate in other activities. You'll have to two sets of bosses - those at the university and those at Westgate. You'll need to wear a suit.

With those difficulties come some bonuses. You'll be given free or cheap accommodation (depending on location), you'll have a very short commitment to decide whether or not life in Japan is for you, and you'll get a work visa (did I mention that already?).

I once applied for a position with Westgate, and had a good experience with the process. I submitted my resume via an online form and wrote a cover letter explaining my experience and goals. After a couple of days, I received an email thanking me for my application and requesting references, which I provided. We arranged a phone interview, which was very friendly and relaxed. The interviewer answered my questions about the program openly, and I was offered a job.

At the time, I was looking for longer-term employment, and though Westgate will renew contracts, there is no salary for the long summer and winter vacations.

I should also point out that Westgate will sometimes hire candidates that it cannot place immediately. Usually, these candidates are offered jobs for the following semester.

This is not a professional career track, but it's definitely an opportunity to get here and gain experience. Though Westgate wasn't the best option for me, it is a very good chance for some people who are uncertain about how to get over here in the first place. It also fits perfectly into the one-two strategy of finding a gateway job and then searching for your desired position form within Japan.

IT AND TECHNICAL JOBS

This is going to be a short chapter, because to be honest, I don't know much about working in this field. Though I love technology and dabble in code (I even went to a technical college), I've always felt my calling was in education and management. Still, the principles of finding and applying for jobs in Japan are going to be the same as what I'll describe elsewhere in this Guide.

If you are an IT pro and looking for work in Japan, here are a few points you should consider.

- **Intracompany Transfer** - This is by far the easiest way to get a technical job in Japan. If your company has an office over here, or has a partnership with a Japanese company, you can request a transfer. The great things about such a situation are that you already have the job, and your company can handle details such as visa and living arrangements.
- **Competition** - Your biggest disadvantage with now is the huge amount of competition for technical positions. This is a hot industry being pushed heavily by schools in Japan and neighboring countries in Asia. Many of these jobs are held by young Chinese immigrants who speak Japanese and can work for relatively little money. Experience is a key factor when competing in such a market.
- **Language Skills** - Most Japanese techies can read some level of English, but very few will be able to speak it well. Learning some Japanese and taking the JLPT (see Advanced Qualifications) can be a huge help here.
- **Qualifications** - Since there are so many people who can do technical work in Japan, you'll need to differentiate yourself to land a good position. In some fields, you'll need to prove that you have over

ten years of experience to even be granted a visa. Certifications and qualifications relevant to your field can also help.

There are actually a good number of positions available, and most of them are advertised online. Check the Resources section so you know where to look, as these jobs are not typically posted on the same sites as those focused on the TEFL industry.

OTHER OPTIONS

This guide is focused in landing teaching jobs in Japan, because that's the most common option. Don't get the wrong idea that it's the only option though. Japan is a modern country, and there are any number of employment options. If you have the experience and skills, you can find and secure employment in almost any field in Japan. To illustrate the variety of options available, I want to highlight a couple of opportunities that don't really qualify as "jobs," but could be interesting nonetheless.

Temple Stays

The first option is staying in Buddhist temples. Many temples will accept visitors for stays, and this can be done on a tourist visa since no money is exchanged.

This can be a great way to experience a side of Japan that most Japanese even never experience. You will live with the monks by the rules of the temple and participate in the daily rituals. This may include periods of silence, meditation at certain times of day, a special (sparse) diet, cleaning chores, and time for reflection. If you're into an ordered way of life and lots of quiet time, this is a serious option.

In many temples, you can stay for a few days or even several months. I've heard of several cases in which visitors were able to renew tourist visas with a little help from the head abbot to continue their study of Zen and simple lifestyle.

If you are considering this approach, make sure you do your research. You will have to adopt the way of life of a monk. Nothing wrong with that at all, but you should know what you're getting into. The best way to get more information about temples and monasteries that accept foreign visitors for extended stays is to contact the Kyoto Tourism Board. Kyoto is the cultural capital of Japan and home to hundreds of temples. Often, you can arrange a visit via email and work out the details from there.

Volunteering

There are various volunteering opportunities in Japan that can be discovered with a simple Google search. One of the larger and better organized programs is through World Wide Opportunities on Organic Farms. WWOOF offers free room and board in exchange for working at one of a number of locations in rural Japan. Openings are listed on the website (see Resources) and can include a variety of jobs.

Volunteering in such an environment can be a good way to see how real people live outside of Japan's massive cities. You'll work closely with other volunteers and staff and have the chance to build strong relationships. It can be a very special experience doing meaningful work and meeting interesting people. Of course, it doesn't pay, but I've heard that the best things in life are free anyway.

Do be aware, however, that some volunteer programs are not free to join. In many cases, there is a registration or membership fee that can range from very reasonable to "I have to pay to be able to work?" Most of the more reliable options will not require you to pay more than a few bucks, so don't worry too much about it. Just do your research.

If you're interested in volunteer opportunities, be sure to check the Resources section and find out what programs are available.

Leverage

So why am I really including these non-jobs in a guide to finding jobs? Because they both give you a way to come to

Japan and make contacts while learning Japanese language and culture.

If there is any one principle in this Guide that I would label as more important than the others, it would be that finding quality employment is a matter of communication above any other consideration. You have to communicate your strengths and benefits to any potential employer in order to receive an offer. How you communicate your cultural vacation or volunteer activities in Japan to recruiters can make a huge difference in your appeal.

Learning to leverage even non-paid experience into a real job that includes visa sponsorship may sound like a hell of a leap, but it's not impossible when you combine your other education and experiences with a good attitude and professional appearance.

Take any chance you have to spend time in Japan and learn about it, because your genuine interest and willingness to try new things will be huge selling points in your campaign for employment in Japan.

DUE DILIGENCE

One of the harsh realities you will run into as a foreign employee in Japan is that you are a foreign employee. I hate to be the one to tell you, but this is not a position of power in Japan.

Although there are unions and labor laws here, and they do cover foreign workers, they are set up for Japanese nationals. The laws are written in Japanese (just like your official contract). Beyond that, you may find that many Japanese people have the attitude to "just shut up and deal with it" when things aren't right. This goes for violations of their own rights as well as yours, so don't expect much sympathy and assistance from Japanese friends if you think you are getting a raw deal.

It's a sad reality that there are companies and schools here that care much more about their profits than they do about your happiness. Shocking, I know. Now get this: these companies may engage in questionable practices that are designed to tilt the balance in their favor rather than yours.

Of course, every company exists to make a profit, but there are levels and degrees between understandable and outrageous. The fact is that *integrity* is strictly a Western value, and you will find that the outside appearance of a school can often differ significantly from the reality of working there.

So what do these companies do that is so bad? Well, it's all relative. Some of them advertise a high salary which turns out to be contingent on "bonuses" that are next to impossible to earn. Some of them include national holidays in the number of days off they promise in their contracts.

Honestly, most of these issues can be identified before you sign a contract. But sometimes, you'll hear of a particular school that seems to be going out of its way to make life suck for the poor, poor native English teachers. In the past, one had no way of knowing whether or not the contract they were about to sign was from one of these schools. Then Al Gore invented the internet, and we began to communicate.

Now there are quite a number of us foreign employees living in Japan. As our numbers and knowledge have grown, we've established systems for protecting ourselves against these bad situations (because we've given up on help from the Japanese).

One of these systems is the "blacklist."

Blacklists

It's not a new concept, and there are various blacklists online for all number of things. The kind that interests us are the blacklists of Japanese English schools, recruiters, and other companies that hire foreign workers. The two best blacklists you should look over are the ones hosted on ESLcafe forums and at debito.org. Both are listed in the Resources section.

These lists are usually put together by a number of people who have had a good deal of experience living and working in Japan. They are assembled manually from collected forums, blogs, emails, and news media, and they can help you find out if that great offer you just got is something you can rely on or not.

Blacklist information can be extremely useful to a first-timer because first-timers are usually the easiest prey for bad companies. If you are searching for jobs and starting to compare offers, I definitely suggest checking out some of these lists to get an idea of how much you want to trust any promises any particular company makes.

When you check out the blacklists, be careful not to take them for gospel. There are two reasons for this:

    1.   The information may be out of date

2. People on internet forums have a tendency to bitch and moan

There is a Mexican restaurant I used to go to all the time in my hometown. It's still there and has been serving the best burritos and margaritas in town for over twenty years. A few years ago, somebody got sick after eating there and really went after them. If you google the restaurant and city now, you'll still see a few pages advising people to stay away - because one person got sick - in over twenty years!

Personally, I think that's a pretty good track record (better than Taco Bell, at least). It's really a shame that people are steered away from having some of the best food in town because somebody had a bad experience a few years back.

My point is that, maybe a company screwed an employee once (and keep in mind that there are two sides to every story). This does not mean that they are evil bastards out to take advantage of you. If you see a negative post about a company, look into it, but take it with a grain of salt. It's quite possible that an isolated incident has been blown out of proportion by an angry ex-employee who got fired for showing up to work hungover one time too many. You never know.

It's too easy to anonymously "blacklist" a company or school on an internet forum. Don't take somebody with a low post count and a handle like "drunk santa" as an authoritative source, and you should be fine.

Remember: one post is a claim, two are a rumor, and three should be cause to dig deeper.

That said, there are bad companies out there. There are schools that are built around bringing over fresh, naive teachers, using them up , and spitting them out. They make their money by swindling their students and lying to their staff. It's reprehensible to say the least, and they should be avoided.

Most of these schools will have some verifiable history of offense. You can find examples cited on multiple websites and from multiple authors. The claims are specific and factual rather than vague and bitter ("Don't ever work for X, INC., because they're, like, really bad, and they never gave me my last paycheck").

There are a few good resources for blacklist information. You can google "japan English blacklist" or hit up ESL Cafe forums. For a comprehensive college and university blacklist (alongside a corresponding "greenlist," which I think is a really good indicator of fairness), go to Arudou Debito's (aka Dave Aldwinckle's) site. Both of these sites are indexed in the Resources chapter.

ADVANCED QUALIFICATIONS

If you spend any time online searching job boards and information on teaching in Japan, you're bound to eventually come across ads for various teaching certifications. There are several flavors of certification and degrees of trustworthiness of the businesses that sell them.

Before moving on, I want to make it clear that I am a believer in education. I think learning new skills and refining your technique is one of the best ways to invest in yourself in life. If you are serious about a trade or industry and know that you want to make it a lifelong pursuit, spending the time and money to learn about it in a professional and enriching setting can only have positive benefits.

On the other hand, education is a huge industry, and the people who teach these courses are not doing it to better humanity. They do it to make money. It would be a mistake to believe all the seemingly well-intentioned "advice" (aka sales pitches) online when it comes to the necessity of advanced qualifications for teaching positions.

As far as the Japanese government is concerned, the minimum requirement to teach English in Japan is 12 years of formal education in English. However, you need a 4-year degree to get an "Instructor" visa (there are a lot of loopholes various companies use to hire teachers on other visa types, but Instructor is the *proper* visa for anyone teaching for a living). You'll find that, without a college degree, you're going to have very limited options for legal employment here.

To be honest, the actual qualifications vary from job to job. Some companies will hire people who have not graduated college. Most require at least a BA or BS. Universities tend to require an MA or PhD. Private and international schools vary widely in their requirements. Smaller conversation schools may only care that you have a clear accent and don't look Asian.

My advice here is to think about what the requirements are for the jobs you are likely to get. If this is your first time living and working in Japan, I would recommend starting with an entry level position that doesn't require advanced certification. If you then decide that you love life and work here, you can begin to look around at the opportunities you wish to pursue and what qualifications they require.

Remember that education is an investment, and you want to make sure you see a good return on that investment. If you're not going to work in international schools or Japanese universities long term, you might consider investing your time and money in other skills and activities that will give you a better return.

Advanced Qualifications that May or May Not be Useful

MA

The classic advanced certificate in almost any field is the Master of Arts degree. In Japan, this is usually the minimum requirement for teaching at a university. There are some programs that will hire you "part time" without an MA, but getting a contract with and actual university will require an MA or PhD in a field related to whatever you are going to teach. In the case of English, this can mean a degree in English, teaching English as a foreign language, or even education.

It's also possible to teach subjects besides English if you have the qualifications and the university has an international focus. In such a case, most universities will want to see a publications list and a full CV before even discussing the specifics of the position.

I know a few junior high teachers with MAs in TEFL and education, but they don't make more money than their counterparts with BAs. Also know that an MA does not guarantee job placement - I was once chosen for a position in which I was the only candidate *without* an MA, because I had more experience with children.

If you are considering an MA (or PhD), know that it will not open very many doors for you in the job market here in Japan (or really anywhere else, for that matter). It is a serious accomplishment that signifies dedication to a field, and I encourage you to consider it if you're interested in furthering your own education. Just understand that only a few positions in Japan will care either way about those two extra years of schooling.

CELTA
The Certificate of English Language Teaching to Adults is an international certification and generally well-regarded. It is required by some private schools and international schools. Certain dispatch companies also prefer candidates with CELTA certification, but they are by no means required for most teaching positions.

CerTESOL
The Certificate in Teaching English for Speakers of Other Languages is the second major international certificate. It's generally equivalent to the CELTA.

Other Stuff
If you look around online, I'm sure you can find some kind of certificate that isn't covered here, and I'll just advise you to not bother with it unless you have a good reason. Many of these programs are offered in third-world countries and with no accreditation. Though they may try to lure you with promised of "guaranteed job placement," I'd be suspicious without knowing more details about the job being offered.

The Certification that Improves your Quality of Life

JLPT

The Japanese Language Proficiency Test is the one qualification that I recommend for almost everyone, if for no other reason than that they encourage you to study and improve your communication skills. There are four levels of the test.

- **1 kyu** - This is the top level, and it signifies a familiarity and mastery of the Japanese language that meets or exceeds that of most native college graduates. There are almost 2,000 kanji characters tested and some very tricky grammar.
- **2 kyu** - 2 kyu is what people mean when they refer to "business level" Japanese. It requires vocabulary and grammatical knowledge roughly equivalent to that of a high school student, with over 1000 kanji required and a good number of formal expressions.
- **3 kyu** - This level is often called "conversational Japanese," though it isn't adequate for having conversations about much of anything besides the weather and what you plan to eat for breakfast. There are less than 300 kanji tested and some basic reading and essential grammar.
- **4 kyu** - The lowest level of the JLPT is not really useful for anything beyond checking your early progress with the language. There are a few rudimentary kanji, some greetings and idioms, and simple grammar.

Having taken the JLPT can only improve your life overall in Japan. You'll be able to read and speak better Japanese if you study thoroughly. Companies like candidates who can communicate well in Japanese and the JLPT demonstrates that skill. If you plan on spending more than a year or so in Japan, I highly recommend studying for and taking this certification.

There are some excellent resources for studying for and taking the JLPT online, and I've listed a few of the best in the Resources section.

SEARCHING FOR JOBS ONLINE

If you are not already in Japan, and even if you are, the internet is your best friend when it comes to searching for employment in Japan (or indeed, anywhere). There are a ton of job boards and directories specifically covering jobs in Japan. Some resources are centered on English teaching work, but there are other sites that list jobs in a variety of categories.

I have listed the best sources for classifieds and job ads in the Resources section. This section is going to focus on the overall process of finding and applying for a job online.

Look Around

The first thing you should do it to look around at what's out there. Get a feel for some of the job boards and how they work. You'll notice that there are two basic kinds of postings: those for specific positions and those for companies that are recruiting for many positions. The latter posts are often paid and you will typically notice banner ads from those companies on the site (incidentally, those ads are *not* cheap - keep that in mind when you are comparing salaries...).

You'll notice right away that some sites are easier to search and use than others. You'll also find that some companies post the same ads across several sites. This can be handy in certain cases.

Compare Offerings

Now comes the hard part: sifting through all the postings for that magic combination of pay, time, location, and qualifications.

Residence

I'll discuss other qualifications below, but some positions will require candidates already live in Japan. There are several reasons this could be the case, but usually, it's because they need the position filled within a short span of time. Candidates form overseas have to go through the lengthy visa acquisition process before they can begin working, so some companies try to hire form within Japan for certain positions.

Pay

Pay is probably given the most consideration by job seekers, and with good reason. You need money to live, and you are going to have to spend some money to get moved over here. Hence, a high-paying job is very attractive. You'll quickly notice some trends after viewing a few ads. Quite a few of the larger employers will advertise salaries in about the same basic range.

One reason for this is that, the minimum salary allowed for full-time (over 30 hours per week) employment used to be fixed at 250,000 yen per month. Of course, this is before taxes (roughly 10%), insurance (9000 - 25,000 yen per month), and any other deductions (see Your Contract for details). Some places will advertise a slightly higher or lower salary, but this typically includes things like transportation bonuses and other benefits.

At this point, it would be a mistake to discount a company because their posted salary is slightly lower than others. Do however be wary of any position offering *significantly* lower salary without a very good explanation of what benefits you receive instead.

Also note that some companies will not pay you for summer and winter holidays. Some companies do. You'll need to ask.

Time

You should also pay attention to the working days and hours. Most school and office positions are Monday to Friday 8ish to 5ish. English conversation schools will have classes from

Monday to Saturday beginning in the early afternoon and lasting until later in the evening. Your actual working schedule could be any combination of shifts within that window.

Also be aware that there is no guarantee that your days off will be consecutive. You may get Sunday and Wednesday off, or Monday and Tuesday. Or your days off will be different each week.

Some conversation schools make schedules that include a short morning session with very young kids and a medium length session of English conversation later in the evening. In such a case, you would have the afternoons between session off.

There are many different schemes for arranging schedules, so make sure you consider how you're going to structure your personal affairs around your work schedule. Compare the relative convenience of the schedule with the salaries on offer.

Note that there are some four-day-a-week positions with lower pay out there. Some for three days too. If you can live on less money and want to extra time to pursue hobbies, these can be viable for you. But remember that, since you'll be working part time, you'll need to pay for your own insurance, and it may not be possible to find visa sponsorship for part time work.

Location
Finally, remember that salary is relative to expenses. If you are going to live in a city, your rent and other costs of living will probably require around 150,000 to 200,000 yen per month or more. Living in the country can be much cheaper for housing, but may require a car for transportation. Be sure to consider all of these factors when applying.

Also, you may have your own reasons for preferring to live in a certain area of the country. When I was applying for my last job, my primary considerations were being able to live in Northern Osaka and teaching at a public school. Location and hours were the most important factors to me then because I was trying to create a stable situation that would be conducive to my then girlfriend and I getting married. We chose Osaka simply because we wanted to live someplace we hadn't been before, and we were both tired of the countryside.

You may really want to live near Tokyo. I personally suggest experiencing life outside of Japan's larger cities, but this Guide isn't about my preferences, it's about finding the right job for you (eventually) in Japan. Remember to be flexible if you are applying without experience. If you get over here and "do your time," you'll find that you have much greater options down the road.

Qualifications
Besides the residency qualification mentioned above, there are other factors to consider. The basic minimums you will see online are for a BA in any field. That's because you will probably need to prove that you have this in order to obtain a proper work visa. In certain fields, you'll need to show that you have a certain number of years of experience.

Some positions may require, or look favorably on, additional certifications, such as CELTA. I would not recommend investing the time or money in these courses unless you are certain that TEFL is a career you seriously want to pursue. Don't be discouraged if an ad mentions such qualifications - as long as it's not *required*, you can still apply.

The only other very common qualification is experience. Experience is very useful, but chances are, you don't have it unless you're already in Japan. Remember that, in many situations, *related experience* can be just as good if you can sell it. In your cover letter and resume, be sure to describe the ways in which the experience you do have is similar to the position to which you are applying.

Entry level jobs are available. Do not be worried if you don't seem to meet the qualifications posted on some ads. There are others, and you can certainly find someone to hire you.

Weighing Options

I recommend applying to any advertised position that seems appropriate. Without seeing a contract or talking to a company representative, it's difficult to make decisions. You'll need to see know all the factors to weigh the pros and cons of any particular position. You should also consult forums and blacklists to get more information about companies and cities. Get as much information as possible.

Remember that there are lots of different people with different needs and goals. Ultimately, you'll need to decide for yourself what positions will best suit you. Trust your ability to make that decision skillfully, no matter what you read online. As long as you do your research, your informed choice will always be the best it can be.

Finding Back Doors

If you are not located in Japan, you may be feeling a little demoralized upon seeing that so many of the positions advertised on the job boards require you to already be in Japan with a work visa. In some cases, you can still get hired by submitting a resume through the back door - via email. This approach can work partly because it's kind of old school and relies on personal contact.

Even companies that only advertise to applicants already in Japan are capable of sponsoring visas for the right candidates. You just need to get in touch. Find their company website and hunt for an email address and a phone number. You may have to do some googling, but you can usually find a homepage with direct contact information. Use the information in the Resumes and Cover Letters section to build a communication strategy.

The idea is simple: make contact and then find out what possibility you have of getting a position with this company. If it's a larger company, you may try to call on different days to talk to different members of the recruiting department. Get as much info as you can and ask to whom you can submit your resume directly.

Take Something Temporary

It's also entirely possible that you just won't be able to find an excellent job that you are qualified for using the job boards. In such a case, I suggest looking for temporary employment that will give you some experience. Take another look at the Strategy section and consider options such as Westgate's three month teaching contract (which earns you a visa and teaching experience in Japan) or unpaid positions as an intern or volunteer (that allow you to gain experience in Japan, as well as valuable contacts, while visiting on a tourist visa).

Remember that there is no guarantee or even necessity of hitting a home run on your first attempt. There are many options, though, and with perseverance, you *can* find a job in Japan. Once you have *a job*, you can begin to work at getting a *better* job.

FIRST CONTACT

After you have done your shopping and found a few prospective employers offering positions that interest you, it's time to make contact.

Many employment ads will specify the preferred method of contact. Some will list an address, website, email, and phone number. Others will simply direct you to a form. If there are specific instructions given, follow them, but also keep in mind that any information provided is there for your use.

For example, if the ad asks you to fill out a from to express interest but lists a phone number, I would suggest calling first. Talk to someone and ask questions about the company or the positions available. Don't ask questions that are already answered on the website (because then you're wasting their time), but do ask for clarification of any aspects of the position you'd like to know more about. You'll probably still need to fill out the form, but now, when they see your form submission, they will know you from your phone conversation. That makes the form more "real" and makes your application more viable.

In most cases, your first contact will be a resume and cover letter. I've supplied a good bit of detail on both of those in their respective chapters. You will most likely submit them via email or by the interface of an online job board. In either event, you can still call if a phone number is listed (even if it's only listed on the website).

The key with first contact is to try to establish your identity in the minds of the recruiters. Phones are great for this, as are personal emails. Be sure to follow all application instructions if given, but don't be afraid to go the extra mile and make contact personally if possible too. It can really make a difference.

RESUMES AND COVER LETTERS

OK. I'll be honest here and say that the art of resume writing is a very deep subject and well beyond the scope of this course. I am not a resume expert, and I simply cannot teach you how to write the ultimate resume.

Fortunately, a great resume is really not necessary.

For one thing, most of your competition won't have a great resume. For another, many companies won't even look at your resume. Using online forms via websites and email is becoming increasingly common because it allows recruiters to easily enter all your data into spreadsheets and get a clear picture of how you stack up against other candidates.

It used to be that a great resume could differentiate one from competitors by demonstrating unique qualities. That's still true in many industries in the West, but it's just not the way things work in Japan.

Most resumes in Japan are hand-written using forms sold at convenience stores. No joke. It's called a *rirekisho*, which means work history. It has spaces for your school info, prior jobs, a photo, reference contact info, and any questions you have about the position. Don't worry - you won't have to use one of these. I'm just telling you this to show that Japanese companies don't put as much stock in resumes as we tend to in the West. Some Japanese recruiters I've spoken to admit to only scanning the resume and comparing the photos of prospective candidates. (I'll get to photos in another section.)

So the point is, your resume does not have to be "killer." However, that does not mean you can submit anything you like. There are still some guidelines and best practices you should follow to ensure that your resume is well-received.

You probably have a good idea of how to write a resume, and there are plenty of free web resources on doing so. You should make sure in include your name, contact info, education (college and beyond), work history (relevant positions), and skills. Don't include your summer job at Starbucks (unless you were a manager), your high school marching band, or anything that doesn't show you as a professional.

Resume Guidelines

Throughout your resume, you want to focus on using *verbs*. Most people try to write a resume and end up with a lot of adjectives: I'm proficient in working in busy environments because I'm outgoing and efficient." No, no, no.

Show, don't tell. If you are "proficient" at something, give us a concrete example of your proficiency. If you work in a "busy" environment, give us some numbers. How many customers did you serve on an average shift? Show us that you are outgoing and efficient by describing how you increased sales and reduced costs. I think you get the idea.

Since you're applying for a position in another country, you also have to think about the kinds of qualities recruiters may want from an international hire. Adaptability, patience, diplomacy, cultural sensitivity. The abilities to communicate and work with others in challenging environments.

Is this a teaching position? List any teaching experience you have, even if it was unpaid. Can you work with children? Some schools have students ranging in age from two to 70.

Have you done much traveling? If you can adapt to two weeks in Brazil, you can probably adapt to life in Japan. Describe how you learned to communicate and fit in.

Finally, describe your skills. Language skills are great. List any language you have familiarity with. It shows you can learn other languages, and it could be an asset to a school where there are immigrant communities. If you are skilled with computers, sports, or music, include those, as many schools have sports and music activities, and computer skills are always in demand.

With all of these things, remember to focus on showing and using verbs. Write about outcomes and accomplishments that demonstrate your skills.

All of this should fit nicely on one page.

Tailoring

You should also probably write a separate resume for each position for which you intend to apply. The reason for this is that most companies have slightly different needs and wants. You want to make sure your resume is tailored directly to the recruiters' specific candidate wish lists.

How do you do that? Look at the job ad, recruiting page, company website, etc. The language the company uses in their recruiting materials will give you a big hint as to what they are looking for in candidates. Try to mimic some of their wording in your resume (but go easy on this) and play up the angles they seem to be making a point of.

For example, one school website mentions cultural events with students and faculty. They would love to have a new teacher with travel experience. Another company mentions that they provide professional training to corporations like Mitsubishi. They would be more interested in a candidate with corporate or sales experience.

The basic info on your resume won't change (education, work experience), but the way you describe it might. A small company is going to want to know that you are friendly and flexible. A large dispatch company also wants to see flexibility, but is more interested in professionalism and relevant experience. A company that places a large number of candidates doesn't care if you love music, but a private kindergarten will practically require you to sing.

Recruiting materials are usually written by the recruiting department (big surprise, right?), so this is the best chance you have to get inside the minds of the people who are going to be interviewing you. Figure out what they value and deliver it by tailoring your resume for that company.

Keep in mind, I'm not encouraging you to exaggerate the particulars of your skills and experience. I do want you to pay attention to what the recruiters are asking for and highlight those things in your resume.

In many cases, you will just be asked to fill out a web form and won't have a chance to send your actual resume. Many of the larger companies have started making everyone apply via automated systems.

However, the same rules still apply. Answer each prompt so as to best show your specific selling points for that company. Don't get tripped up: "name, address, passport number, duties at last job, personal mission..." Just because you are filling in a form does not mean that you should reply with a laundry list like "took orders, washed dishes." Have your resume handy when you fill out such forms so you can make sure your responses are well-worded and appropriate to your aspirations.

Cover Letters

Finally, we come to the cover letter. A lot of people blow it here.

A cover letter is what gets someone to bother looking at your resume. Most companies will expect a cover letter, and even many automated recruiting systems have a place to include one. The cover letter is your first impression, so don't make it a single line or informal.

A good cover letter template

Date

Name of Employer
Department

Dear Sir or Madam:

Opening: Your goal is to catch the attention of the reader. Clearly state the purpose of writing this letter, including the position or type of work for which you are applying. Indicate how you found out about the position.

This is the most important part of the cover letter. It contains the specific reasons why you want to work for this particular employer. You are marketing yourself here, so you need to draw from your experiences, education and personality to show you are the best person for this position. If you have any specific experience that lends itself well to this particular job, elaborate briefly on its importance.

Closing: Ask for an interview. Your main objective is to get an interview with the company or organization. You can indicate to the individual that you will call on a specific date to set up an appointment. If possible, try to take some control of your application. If you wait for the company to reply, you may never hear from them again. It's best to establish a strategy and set deadlines. When you follow through, it lets the recruiter know that you are serious and dependable.

Sincerely,

[sign]

Your name

Please see attached resume. (Don't forget to include your resume and other requested materials with this cover letter.)

As with the resume, you can tailor your cover letter contents to the specific position. You don't want to mention everything you list on your resume, but you do want to paint a broad picture of your experiences and skills and how they pertain to the position in question. Think of the cover letter as a chance to introduce a narrative about your career path that gets detailed in the resume. Doing this well ensure that your resume will be read thoroughly.

A cover letter should never be longer than one page, unless you know the recipient directly and have a specific reason for including more than the essentials. Keep on point and keep it professional.

Delivery

If you are sending a print resume via snail mail, make sure to use nice paper and a clean envelope. This is really just common sense, but you want to project a professional appearance in all aspects of your communications.

When sending resumes via email or online forms, you should make sure you cater to the needs of your audience, so be sure to set your page attributes (or page setup, etc.) so the paper size is A4. A4 is a standard paper size in most of the world, but it's slightly off from the "letter" size used in America. Make sure your resume will format and print correctly on A4, or you may end up with a jumbled, unreadable resume.

The last point about format is this: make it easy. Do not send your resume in a format that requires a specific type of computer to open. Some companies will accept .doc format from Microsoft Word, but there can still be problems across different versions of this program (and don't expect for a second that the average Japanese office computer runs the newest version of Windows - my last office was still running Windows 2000). Also note that Macs are gaining popularity here, but are by no means common.

To prevent any confusion, make sure you save a copy of your resume in .pdf format. .pdf (or Portable Document Format) will print on almost any computer without any screw-ups. Definitely follow instructions on resume format, but if you aren't given explicit demands to send in X format, .pdf is your best bet.

There are tons of free internet guides to writing resumes, but remember that they are not optimized for getting a job in Japan. Filter any general resume advice you read through the suggestions above, and you'll be ahead of the pack.

Overall, just remember that resumes and cover letters will be how prospective recruiters judge you until they have the pleasure of meeting you in person. Be careful with how you present yourself on paper, and you can be certain you'll have the opportunity to impress them in an interview.

YOUR PHOTO

I'll come right out and make this as clear as I can: Japan is a very image-centered society.

I've heard people call Japanese culture "superficial," and I have a hard time arguing. It's not really that people are shallow so much as the social structure is ... well, let's not get into a sociological discussion. I studied sociology in university, and I could go on and on about this, but the thing you need to know is that your professional image is extremely important to prospective employers.

Yes, there may be exceptions. Yes, there are many Japanese people who wear extremely odd clothing, but you won't find them in the kinds of jobs you are likely to be looking for here. There are also foreign teachers who have dyed hair and piercings. But I can guarantee you that their employers wish they didn't.

This isn't to say that you can't find work if you have tats or whatever. I do advise you to think very carefully about how important is to you that you work someplace that allows you to fly your freak flag. At the very least, consider trying to look as normal and clean cut as possible for your interview.

Likewise for your resume photo.

That's right, you will almost certainly be asked for a photo to even be considered for employment in Japan. In the West, we have to at least pretend that hiring decisions are made on the strict basis of qualifications, but Japanese companies have no qualms about specifying the sex, age, race, height, and weight of their ideal candidates.

Like it or not, in Japan, it's perfectly acceptable (and not uncommon) for a company to hire or reject an applicant based on the photo submitted with the resume. This boils down to one thing: you need a good photo.

Now don't let me give you the wrong impression either. Most employers are far more concerned with who you are and what you know than they are with how you look. However, this is one of those things that can mean the difference between you and a similarly qualified candidate, so it's best to be prepared with your best.

You need to have some passport sized photos made that conform to the following guidelines:

- plain background
- clear shot of head and top portion of shoulders
- clean and neat appearance
- no visible tattoos
- no large earrings (and guys should really consider ditching any jewelry all together)
- a clean shave for the men (or a very, very neatly groomed beard or 'stache)
- for ladies, hair nicely styled and not covering the face (consider pulling it back)
- short hair is preferred for men, but you could get away with longer hair if it is neat and clean
- business attire (ties and jackets for gentlemen, something classy for the ladies)
- a smile
- good eye contact directly into the camera

All of these things make you look like a friendly, healthy, happy professional, which is what most companies are looking for. (Just imagine a group of recruiters talking about how they'd love to find a sickly, depressed, jerk to fill a position...) Try to imagine their dream employee and figure out how you can look as much like that person as possible.

But don't go overboard. You still want to be yourself. Don't be afraid to show some personality. You don't have to wear a black suit with a grey tie. Just remember that you want to show your personality in your smile and facial expression more than your clothes.

After you take your photos, feel free to dress how you like. I won't tell.

Honestly, you shouldn't stress out over this, but you do want to make sure that you are presenting the best image of yourself to anyone who may hire you.

REFERENCE LETTERS

As a general rule, prospective employers in any country will look for candidates with strong references. This is the origin of the saying "It's not what you know; it's who you know."

While it's not necessary to have an "in," it can certainly help, and references are your chance to at least show that you have connections *somewhere*. If that somewhere is a school or a Japanese business, you have a definite advantage here, because ideally, your references should be relevant to the position for which you are applying. Positive reviews of your performance in similar positions are a good indicator that you can perform in this position.

However, if you are applying without the benefit of prior experience, you can still find someone to write a winning recommendation. To get a better idea of how to do that, let's first look at what reference letters need to accomplish.

A good reference letter does a couple of things. First, it shows that the writer knows the candidate well enough to make a recommendation. It should mention that you've built a relationship over some period of time in which you have adequately demonstrated your desirable characteristics. Second, it should establish what those characteristics are and how you put them to use.

So basically, you need to think of someone you've developed a working relationship with who can shed some light on how you've contributed your particular skills and qualities to a successful project.

This can really be almost anybody you aren't related to or dating. University professors, church group leaders, organizers for events at which you've helped out, coaches, mentors, former supervisors, professional trainers, etc., are all good choices. The key is that this person can make a case for your unique talents and abilities in a specific context.

Nobody is going to hire you because you're friendly, unless you're applying for a greeter position at Wal-Mart. Make sure your reference understands the qualities you want to impress upon the letter's recipients. Don't be shy about telling them precisely what you want them to include or exclude from the letter. After all, it's your future we're talking about here. To be honest, most people feel a heavy responsibility when asked to provide letters of recommendation, so you'll actually be doing a them a big favor by giving them some guidelines.

The Guidelines

- Be succinct
- Focus on the candidate's unique qualities (some qualities recruiters look for are: adaptability, creativity, leadership, ability to work on a team, initiative, positivity, open mindedness, responsibility)
- Describe how those qualities lead to success in a competitive environment or difficult situation.
- Describe ways in which the candidate went beyond your expectations to deliver excellent results.

And that's really it. A reference letter should not dwell on who you are, but instead needs to focus on how you've demonstrated the ability to contribute to a particular project. Also, ask your references to resist any urge to conjecture on what a good teacher (or whatever) you will probably be - that's the recruiter's job. Have your references stick to what they know: how great you are. If they do a good job of that, recruiters will have no difficulty seeing you as a member of their company.

Again, feel free to tell your references what you'd like them to mention. If you are focusing on your experience in organizing an event or handling customer complaints, you want your reference to highlight your abilities in those situations.

Some things you may ask a reference to write about:

- Day-to-day activities or work duties (if they are relevant)
- School extracurricular activities
- Volunteer activities
- International experience or cultural exchange
- Language skills
- Projects you've managed
- Membership in professional organizations
- Articles you have written
- Other events in which you've participated

The person writing the reference should mention any of the above items that are relevant to his or her relationship with you and feature your talents and skills.

Basic letter format for most situations

Date

Reference for [your name]

To whom it may concern:

Describe writer's current position and relationship with candidate. How long have you been acquainted?

How did you meet? Describe the situation in which you worked together. What challenges did the candidate face?

How did the candidate meet these challenges in a way that impressed the writer? What qualities did the candidate demonstrate that would be assets to the prospective employer?

It was a pleasure working with [candidate] during [whatever period of time], and I can recommend him/her without reservation for any position in which [a couple of the candidate's qualities] are considered assets.

[sign]

Writer's name
position
company

contact information (phone, fax, email)

Of course, some companies may ask for specific information to be included in references, and you'd be foolish not to make sure your letters meet those requirements. In most cases, the above will work just fine. Also make sure that there are no grammatical or factual errors, as these always affect your credibility.

Try to get two strong letters from people you respect. Why do you need to respect this person? Because you may be asked about your relationship and work with them in an interview, and it would be great to be able to tell your interviewers exactly what you learned from the experience your reference is writing so glowingly about. Making your reference look good makes you look good (because they are recommending you). It's easier to do this if you genuinely respect and appreciate them.

For some positions, you may be able to email a copy of the letter. For some positions (JET Programme, for one example), you'll need to have a signed and sealed letter to send with your application package. I recommend having your references sign several copies of their letters in advance so you don't have to bother them with subsequent requests.

Finally, ask your references for permission to give their contact details to prospective employers. Some companies ask to be able to contact references directly, and the last thing you want is for them to be irritated at having to answer questions about you without expecting it. If possible, let them know that x from COMPANY Y is going to be getting in touch about POSITION Z and thank them in advance for their help. Offer to buy them a beer (if that's appropriate to your relationship, of course) to say thanks.

All other things being equal, a candidate with great references has an edge over a candidate with mediocre references. If you don't have much directly related job experience, references are one way to show that you have demonstrated useful skills in the past.

References probably won't make or break your chances if everything else is in place, but they can definitely help give you a little social proof.

INTERVIEWING

The key to securing a job offer is the interview, and the key to passing an interview is preparation. This section is all about preparing you to give a good interview that demonstrates your strengths and shows you as an asset to your prospective employer.

Why do companies want to interview candidates? They want to learn more about you. They want to compare the impression gave in writing (with your application/resume and especially your cover letter) with the impression you give in person. Ideally, these should be the same impression, because this spells integrity and authenticity to a recruiter. You primary job at an interview is to show that all those strengths and goals you listed in your prior contact are actually there in person - that they can be called upon by you to perform on the job.

There are various kinds of interviews. Individual or group. Informal cafe meeting or formal boardroom meeting. You may interview in the company break room over biscuits and tea (as I did with an interviewer from England. I don't drink tea, and as an American, I call those little sweet things "cookies"). You may have a single interviewer, you or may get the panel interview, which most often includes a non-Japanese recruiter (good cop) and a Japanese honcho (bad cop). Some interviewers will try to play games with you and others just want to chat.

In all of these cases, your mom gave the best advice: "Just be yourself, Honey, and everyone will love you."

A Walkthrough

I'll describe some typical interview situations. As you read, keep in mind that any of the above variations will probably share the same key features.

Show up. Show up early. Look good (appropriate to the style of interview. Ask your contact person about this before hand). Go to the bathroom before you arrive. Brush your teeth if you ate recently. You know, don't be a slob.

On arrival introduce yourself to the first person you see and state your business. If you know the name of your interviewer, you should say so. You may have to wait a few minutes, or you may get to go right ahead.

When you meet your interviewer(s), smile and stand straight (not unnaturally straight though). Shake hands. If they bow, you should too (don't worry about how low or any other nonsense). You'll be shown to a seat and possibly offered coffee or tea. You may make small talk for a few minutes. Just be positive and friendly.

There's no reason to be nervous at this stage of the interview (or really any other stage). Try to relax as much as is possible with your clothes on and have a genuine and friendly interaction with the interviewer.

Once some rapport has developed, you'll move on to some easy questions. Most of the questions will be about things not on your resume. If the interviewer knows someone at your college, he may bring it up, but don't expect to talk much about your stats and work history, unless it's very relevant to the position.

If you are well prepared, these questions should be pretty easy. The thing to remember is that it is more about *how* you answer the questions than what you are actually saying. What you say is still important, but your communication skills are a major factor too.

After the basics have been covered, the interviewer will move on to the more interesting questions. Things like career goals, your personal experiences, how you might deal with hypothetical situations, what you expect from the position, etc. Here are a few examples of the kinds of questions you are likely to be asked. Notice that many of them are quite broad.

- Tell me about yourself.
- What are your goals?
- Why do you want to be a _____?
- What can you add to our organization as an employee?
- What are your strengths and weaknesses?
- What was your greatest success?
- What was your greatest failure?
- Why are you more qualified than my other candidates?
- Least favorite task in your last job?
- What salary are you looking for?
- Why do you want to work for this company?
- Where do you see yourself in 5 to 10 years?

These questions are designed to find out as much about you as possible and determine what kind of employee you will be. Keep your answers concise, and expand on anything the interviewer seems to be especially interested in. Don't tell stories unless they are super-relevant. Also avoid making assumptions or generalizations about Japan or the position. Above all, be honest and be yourself.

You'll probably be asked if you have any questions about the company or the position. You probably do, so go ahead and ask them. You should have read the company website and be familiar with their reputation, so ask questions that show you have done your homework. For example, don't ask "what are the benefits for this job?" You should have been given some idea of that before the interview. Instead, ask "does [company name] offer a choice between private or national insurance?" That's a good question that shows you have studied and planned.

A few questions you may consider asking:

- What are the people who held this position previously doing now?
- How much responsibility is given to new employees in this department?
- Upon what criteria are employees in this department evaluated?
- With whom would I work closely in this job?
- Are there opportunities for advancement?
- What are the company's goals for the next few years?
- What types of people succeed in this environment?
- Describe your training program.

Then you'll be done. You can shake hands again and go home, or to a bar, or whatever.

It's usually a good idea to send a follow-up note to thank the interviewer for answering your questions and meeting with you. Keep this short and cordial. Restate your interest in the position and close.

Sample Lessons

One of the really stupid conventions of interviews for English teachers in Japan is the "Sample Lesson." It's like every interviewer went to the same three-day course on HR management and slept through the first two days.

The problem with the sample lesson is that its inclusion in interviews is based on several false premises: that adults can role play the parts of children, that the response from small group can mimic the feedback from a classroom, that a lesson without context can accurately model a lesson that takes place in a real school... Teaching is a dynamic interaction between the instructor(s), students, and material. A solo sample lesson in front of two recruiters is just not going to come close to reproducing the environment of classroom instruction.

Luckily, the sample lesson is not always required, but I've had to do two of them, and they are popular with certain companies.

The things to remember with a sample lesson are to engage the audience and speak in clear and simple English. You should have a very easy activity in mind (check the Resources section) and practice explaining it in language a five year old would understand. You should have a five minute version and a ten minute version.

The number one rule about the sample lesson is not to stress. It's not the most important part of your interview, it's just another part. If you do well in the Q&A portion of the interview, you'll probably be offered a position.

YOUR CONTRACT

Contracts are a giant pain, but they are really important because they spell out the exact conditions of your employment. Some contracts are very loose and general, while others seem to be extremely detailed. I have seen single page contracts and fifteen page contracts for essentially the same job here in Japan. Since you will be bound by any contract you sign, you should pay attention and make sure you know what you're getting into.

I'm not a lawyer, but there are a few things I think you should look for in a contract.

Hours

There are two kinds of hours: onsite hours, and working hours. Your onsite hours may include a lunch break that isn't paid. ALTs will often have 35 onsite hours with 29.5 working hours. Of those, only 12 to 20 will be spent in the classroom. There is no right or wrong number of hours so long as it matches the pay scale. The thing to notice is that, if you work less than 30 hours, you are a part time employee. In such a case, your company is not required to subsidize your health insurance.

Remuneration

That's a fancy word for pay. This is how much you will earn. Note carefully any bonuses included. Some companies advertise a salary of a certain amount that, in reality, includes bonuses. There is no guarantee that you will earn bonuses each pay period, so do not count on receiving anything above your base salary.

The other thing to notice are any deductions. These could be for taxes or benefits such as insurance. If you are using company housing, you may have a deduction for rent. Know how much your first paycheck is going to be in advance so you don't wind up with an unpleasant surprise.

Other Benefits

Certain contracts may offer additional benefits. Make sure to take advantage of these. You may be able to get your return flight reimbursed (or a portion of it) upon completion of your contract terms. In larger cities, it's standard to have a transportation stipend. You may be allowed access to a company car. There are lots of options.

Be sure to check out all of the benefits available to you and weigh their value for you relative to the other conditions.

Accommodation

If you use company housing, it will be addressed in your contract. Pay attention to rules about overnight guests and any penalties should you decide you want to search for better accommodation on your own. If the apartment is furnished, you can save some money, but you'll also be stuck with ugly, used furniture for your tenure there. Be sure to note any mention of utilities and find out if internet is available. You may also have to pay a cleaning deposit or something similar.

Be sure to get the facts about how far the apartment is from your workplace. Is there a place to park a bike or a car (if you plan to have one)? How large are the rooms? Is there a supermarket nearby? Is there storage space for things like suitcases?

All of this stuff is pertinent and important so be sure to read the contract and ask questions before you sign on the dotted line.

Days Off

Certain companies are notorious for advertising national holidays as days off in their employment ads. You must read the contract. Know how many days are in your contract. How many days a year do you work? How many days do you get off for spring, summer, and winter breaks? How many vacation days can you take? It's probably fewer than you think. How many sick days do you have? You may be asked to show proof of a doctor visit.

Know if there are salary deductions for days not worked. Don't make any assumptions about days off, because it's a major sticky issue with many contracts from dispatch companies and the large English conversation schools.

Quitting

Being an American, I feel that I have an inborn right to say the words "take this job and shove it." Sometimes, things don't work out. Sometimes, the employer and employee just do not get along. It happens, and there needs to be a way to address it fairly. Most of the contracts I have seen in Japan did not address this eventuality equitably at all.

For example, I once applied and interviewed for a job with a great little company that seemed like a sweet deal. Everything was going great, and I was given a contract to sign. I began to read it over, and immediately, I got the feeling that something wasn't right. It's hard to explain, but some of the wording just seemed a little too tricky. Towards the end of the contract, there was a clause that essentially said:

"We can fire you for any reason, but you cannot terminate this agreement without reimbursing your entire salary."

What?!?! I asked the hiring manager about the clause and she responded that they could lose money if I decided to end my employment. They would have to replace me to fulfill their obligations to their client, and they didn't have the time or resources to do that. I would simply have to agree to a one-year commitment with no way out. I did not sign that contract.

For the record, you are supposed to be able to quit any job in Japan with a certain amount of prior notice, even if it goes against your contract, but I would not advise signing such a contract in the first place. You may find that companies with tricky contracts will attempt to withhold your final paycheck if you have to leave before the end of your contract (even after giving proper notice).

Or they may just not be very nice. You shouldn't deal with companies that operate like that. Read your contract carefully so you don't get screwed. You *can* find employment with a company that will treat you fairly. Do not settle for exploitation.

Insurance

There is a lot of BS floating around the internet regarding necessary insurance coverage. The laws are pretty complicated, but the key point to keep in mind is that Japan expects you to be insured. In fact, if you plan to be here for over a year, you *must* enroll in one of the two national insurance plans. In the past, some foreign workers have gotten by on private or no insurance, but things have recently gotten much stricter.

The two health insurance plans are *shakai hoken*, which your employer is responsible for subsidizing (thus, it's not very popular with many employers) and *kokumin kenko hoken*, which you must use if you are self-employed or working only part-time.

Here's where it gets tricky: if you are in Japan a for over a year and don't pay into one of these systems, you are not legal. You will not be able to renew your visa without enrolling, and you will be responsible for up to two years of retroactive payments.

My advice - enroll in *shakai hoken* (if your contact provides for it) or *kokumin kenko hoken* as soon as you begin working. They are relatively cheap for the first year of coverage, since the premiums are calculated on your previous year's earnings (which are zero if you've just moved here).

You should also make sure your company enrolls you in *koyou hoken* or employment insurance. It's cheap and can save your ass if you end up without a job.

Ask Questions

If you have any questions about any contract items, you should definitely ask. Also look for any clauses that look as if they are designed to trap you. Ask what their purpose is and how you can protect your interests. You do not need to sign an exploitive contract.

Internet forums related to living and working in Japan are full of people complaining about how COMPANY X cheated them in some way. In 99 cases out of a hundred, these people signed contracts that specifically defined the terms of their employment. If you sign a contract for 29.5 hours, you are a part time employee, and your employer does not have to provide you with insurance coverage unless the contract specifically states that they will. In such a case, you have no right to complain about getting screwed by your employer. You screwed yourself by signing a contract your couldn't agree with.

Don't get the wrong idea here that I'm suggesting to stay away from 29.5 hour contracts or companies that don't provide insurance. If you can live on part time pay (and it's possible in some cases), that's not a problem. There are some relatively cheap private insurance packages available online. For some people, those might be the way to go. What I'm really saying is that you need to know what your contract says and expect that your company will follow it. You'll need to follow it as well.

YOUR VISA
"Don't leave hone without it."

Yes, I know that "Don't leave home without it" was the AmEx slogan, not Visa, but this is important. Let's dive straight into a few visa facts:

- You cannot work in Japan without a visa.
- You cannot get a work visa from within Japan.
- You can get a work visa without a guarantor (your employer), but it is not very likely that your application will be approved.
- You must apply for a visa in person at a Japanese embassy or consular office.

These four facts are sometimes debated online in forums where people try to claim that they've "hacked" Japanese immigration. This kind of shady dealing will likely end in greater expense than moving by legitimate means. Not to mention the possibility of deportation if you are caught trying to beat the system. The Japanese government has really cracked down on illegal immigration in the past few years, and the chances of getting away with working here sans-visa are very slim.

You've been warned.

Kinds of Visas

Now that that's out of the way, we can get to the mechanics of the visa process. Essentially, there are just a few types of visa that one can use to work: spousal visa, one of several classes of work visa, a working holiday visa, or a student visa. I'll outline the details of each below.

Spousal Visas
If you are married to a Japanese national and can show that you live together, you can apply for a spousal visa. Obtaining one is

a fairly simple procedure, given that you have documented proof of your marriage and shared address. Simply visit the consular office and fill out the application.

Remember that visas are not guaranteed to spouses of Japanese. If immigration suspects that there is anything fishy with your situation, they may require additional documentation or deny your application. By "fishy," I mean anything that looks like you are trying to cheat. If you have only been married for a few days (within annulment range, for example) before applying for a visa, "proof" of your relationship (photos, etc.) may be required.

As a side note about relying on a spousal visa to work in Japan, you need to be aware that marriage in Japan is pretty simple. However, divorce is a very difficult thing to achieve, requiring a good deal of time (months) and effort. Also note that, you cannot retain a spousal visa after a divorce.

Work Visas
This is what most people reading this guide will be after. To do this right, you're going to need an employer to act as your guarantor. It's supposedly possible to obtain a working visa otherwise, but you'll need to prove a steady stream of "adequate" income and show that you have a good deal saved as well.

Unfortunately, it takes time and effort for employers to sponsor a visa for you. They have to obtain all of your documents and make an application on your behalf to the regional immigration authority. Actually, it's possible (but not recommended) to do this yourself (though you'll still need a guarantor), but it has to be done from within Japan, and employers can handle it much more efficiently.

There are 14 classes of working visa in Japan, and they each have subtly different requirements. In principle, most working visas will require proof of college or university graduation and a record of work experience. This varies of course. An instructor visa to teach foreign language may only require that you finished your formal education in that language. A visa for business management may require a good deal more in terms of personal background. The specifics are often unique to the situation.

Above, I wrote "...visa to teach English may only require..." The "may" part is because your application will be reviewed by a person, and I've heard a lot of evidence that different people at different immigration offices can interpret various points in different ways. The key is just to provide them with any information they ask for and have faith that your sponsor will eventually find a way to get your application approved.

If you are offered a job and visa sponsorship by an employer, they will put things in motion by applying for a Certificate of Eligibility so you can apply for a visa. You'll need to work with your future employer to provide the required documents and make sure that everything is up-to-date and in-order.

Once you have received the COE (details below), you can apply for a visa by submitting an application and COE together at your nearest embassy or consular office. If you have a COE, you can usually get a visa within a few days. Last time I applied for a visa in Atlanta, it was ready after lunch.

Once you have your visa, you are legally permitted to work in Japan for the duration of the visa, *even if you change employers.*

Working Holiday Visas
At present, Japan has such working holiday agreements with nine countries: Australia, Canada, France, New Zealand, the Republic of Korea, Germany, the United Kingdom, Ireland and Denmark. To get a Working Holiday visa, you need to be between 18 and 30 years old.

As the requirements may differ form country to country, the best thing to do would be to simply call the nearest Japanese embassy or consulate and inquire directly about the procedure for obtaining a working holiday visa.

Student Visas

To get a student visa, you will have to show that you have been accepted by a Japanese university or other eligible school. The school will act as your guarantor and apply for your COE (see below).

Technically, you cannot work on a student visa. Not without permission, anyway. To get that permission, you need to apply for "Permission to Engage in an Activity Other Than That Permitted by the Status of Residence Previously Granted." You can do this by submitting a form at the nearest immigration office.

If permission is granted, you will be allowed to work up to 20 hours per week.

Applying for a Visa

To apply for a visa, you need to take the required documents to a Japanese embassy or consulate along with some money. The necessary documents vary depending on the visa type, but the essentials are:

- Your passport - make sure it's not going to expire anytime soon
- Two 45mm x 45mm photos taken within the previous six months
- A visa application (get it at the office and fill it out there)
- A Certificate of Eligibility of other documentation certifying the purpose of your visit

Certificate of Eligibility

In 99% of all cases, you will need a COE to be granted a visa for work in Japan. You can count on this taking at least a month and up to three months. Why so long? Because Japanese people need jobs, and the best way anyone can think of to provide them is by creating byzantine interagency systems for shuffling of papers.

The COE is applied for from within Japan at a regional immigration office. This is usually handled by your employer if you are applying for a work visa. For a student visa, your guarantor is your school, and they will handle the paperwork for you. In cases of a spousal visa, you could have your in-laws apply on your behalf.

It is also theoretically possible to "self-sponsor" and apply on your own. If you choose to do this, you will need to show that you have stable income and a clean criminal record. You'll also have to visit the regional immigration authority in person and probably be interviewed. This process takes just as long as being sponsored by an employer. That's three months that you will have to be in Japan without the ability to work legally. If you can afford that, you might be able to persuade immigration to approve your application.

Once you have your COE, you are basically home free to obtain a visa. Lucky you.

Applying without a COE
First, don't get your hopes up. Your application will have to be investigated in Japan by the immigration authority. This will probably take a couple of months. You'll also need extra documentation. You'll need a letter from your guarantor. Yes that's right, you still need someone in Japan to vouch for you. You'll also need to show that you have money to cover living expenses if you aren't going to be working.

Now You're Official

If you've gone through the long and tedious process correctly, you'll have a shiny new visa seal affixed inside your passport. It'll include a pixelated photo of you and some writing. Congrats!

Once You Have Your Visa

Take note of the writing on the visa. It expires and has a time period. Most visas will expire in 3 months from the date of issue. This means you need to arrive in Japan within that timeframe. The period of stay is how long after you arrive in Japan you will be permitted to stay.

In most cases, this will be one year for the initial visa. Make plans to apply for an extension before that time. Note that this can be done in one day if you are lucky. It can also take a couple of weeks, or up to a month. If you are planning to remain in Japan beyond the period of your initial visa, you need to plan ahead and get an extension.

One final thing to notice about your visa is the part where it lists the number of entries. This is the number of times you can use this visa to enter Japan. In most cases, it's one. As in, don't think that you can enter and leave Japan freely for the duration of your visa. If you plan to travel outside of Japan, you will need to apply for a re-entry permit at an immigration office. This simple application only takes a couple of hours, but if you neglect it, you could end up in a serious predicament.

START-UP COSTS

Important: You need to bring money to Japan with you!

Except in very rare cases, you will need to have the equivalent of at least $2 - 3,000 US to move to Japan comfortably. More if you are responsible for finding your own apartment. And you'll need to have it in cash.

Honestly, this should really go without saying, but I'm constantly surprised at the number of people who seem to think they can make an international move with no capital. In every Japan-related internet forum, there are tons of questions and comments from people trying to find out if Japan is "really that expensive." The answer is: it depends, but if you have to ask, yes.

It depends because, as the saying goes, every situation is different. However, for 99.9% of people who don't already know exactly what they're getting into, moving to Japan will cost more than expected. You can count on it.

I know people looking to live and work in Japan are specifically doing so because it's a step up from their current careers. Many seeking employment in Japan are recent college graduates. After all, if you were rich, you'd probably be able to just fly over and hang out whenever you felt like it, right? Unfortunately, moving is expensive, and moving to Japan is double expensive. I'm really sorry I have to be the one to tell you.

The thing is, it used to be easier, back in the glory days. It used to be common practice for employers to provide airfare for incoming English teachers. If you are an expert in a technical field, you may still be able to get such a deal, but JET is the only major employer of English teachers that still provides transportation to and from Japan. Everyone else has to find their own way over here, and depending on time of year and fuel prices, that can be quite an investment.

Actually, living in Japan is no more expensive than living in any other industrialized nation. Figuring rent, utilities, food, insurance, and recreation into the equation, most foreign residents I know in Japan are making at least the same money they would be making at home. Well, excluding those of us who gave up professional positions to become English teachers.

Though things in Japan *seem* expensive when compared with other countries, the fact is that other things are cheaper. Life in Japan will also be much more expensive for newbies that haven't learned where to find the bargains yet. As you grow accustomed to life in Japan and learn your way around, the cost of living will drop noticeably. After a year or two, you'll be amazed at how cheaply you can live in Japan while still traveling and having a great time socially. You just have to shop around and plan ahead.

Still, none of that really helps when you're just getting established. Until you get used to things, you're going to waste money on stuff that you just can't figure out how to find for cheap. You'll pay full price for things that Japanese people wait for discounts to buy. You'll catch on eventually and learn to do your grocery shopping near closing time when everything gets marked down. Besides the learning curve, there are several other factors that make the first few months of living in Japan more expensive than you might expect.

The first thing you need to know about money in Japan is that most places prefer cash. Credit is increasing in popularity, but it still isn't universally accepted, especially outside of the cities. You may also run into problems using a foreign-issued card, though this, too, is less of a problem than it used to be. Do keep in mind though that your credit provider will charge an exchange fee and possibly and international transfer fee on top of every transaction you make in Japan. Add interest, and that gets expensive very quickly.

Besides that, there are still things for which you just cannot pay by credit. Cash is king in Japan. You will need plenty of it.

Another thing to consider when planning your initial budget is that you probably won't get paid until you've been here for a couple of months. Assuming you begin work within a week of arrival, it may still be almost two months before you see your first payday. The majority of Japanese businesses pay once a month on a specific date. For example, you may get paid for a month's work on the last day of the following month. You might get paid sooner, but this is something you'll need to check out in your contract before you bet on having income at a particular time.

In some cases, companies will offer interest-free advances to employees who need some financial help to get started. This is a very generous situation, and you have to appreciate that kind of good faith from an employer, but don't forget that this money is going to be deducted from your pay until the debt is clear. Keep in mind that, if you are staying in a company-provided apartment or using a company car, you may have extra deductions and fees taken automatically out of your pay. There may also be deductions for local taxes, insurance, or pension (especially if you are in JET - though you can get some of that back when you leave Japan). Take all of these things into consideration, and don't expect your first paycheck to be anything to write home about.

A final major moving cost that takes many people by surprise when they first move to Japan is the ridiculous amount of cash that's required to secure housing. In addition to a guarantor (usually your employer) who vouches for your ability to pay the rent, you'll have to pay commissions and "key money" to the landlord and agent totaling up to three or four times the monthly rent. You may also need to pay a cleaning deposit. Don't forget your first month's rent and utilities.

Of course, your employer may have you covered on some parts of this. Many dispatch companies contract a large number of apartments so they can provide housing for their employees without the need for key money and commissions.

Most JETs will have very reasonable accommodations provided by their boards of education (but don't count on it). I lived in a very nice house that I paid next to nothing for. A very good friend of mine paid about $500 US for an apartment with no heat or A/C and a bug problem. To make matters worse, she couldn't find a better place because it was specified in her contract. The take home here is to check the conditions of your contract if you employer is providing housing for you.

All contracts are negotiable until they're signed.

If your employer cannot assist you with finding a place to live, be prepared to put down a large sum before you can move in. Up to four or five months rent.

Shoestring Budget

After all that about needing a lot of money, I should confess that, the first time I moved to Japan, I did so with $600 cash and several thousand dollars of credit card debt. Somehow, I did not die. You probably won't either.

The reality is that, in Japan, as with anywhere else, it is possible to get by on a shoestring budget. If you're dedicated. You'll have to skimp on food and avoid going out. It's not exactly the way most people want to experience life in a new place, but it is effective for making your money last. If you have debt to pay off, you can get by on very little here once you've paid your bills.

One of the best resources for learning how to live frugally in Japan is Japanese people. I know that may come as a shock, but you;d be surprised how many people never seem to do the obvious thing...

Ask your coworkers and friends about saving money, and they will be happy to give you loads of advice.

There are many ways to spend money in Japan, or anywhere else for that matter. The good news is that, once you get set up, you can live quite cheaply and comfortably here if you are sane. It's still possible to work really hard for a few years and pay off your school loans (or a large chunk of them) while eating well and still having plenty of fun. But it's not automatic, and you won't be able to save much at first.

Bring as much cash to Japan as you can. You will be glad you did.

STUFF TO DO BEFORE YOU LEAVE

Here are a few things you can do before departing for Japan that will make your life easier.

- Learn Japanese. Even if you have no interest in becoming fluent and plan to teach English, any Japanese you can speak will help you. Most people here do not speak any English at all and have no confidence in their ability to communicate with non-Japanese. Language is a tool, and Japanese language skill is the most useful tool you can have while living in Japan.
- Be aware that there are various dialects of Japanese. While the standard language is understood everywhere, you may be confronted with words you don't understand when you get out of Tokyo. If you're moving to Osaka, for example, I'd suggest buying a guide to *kansaiben*.
- Make sure your passport will not expire for the duration of your stay in Japan. Yes, you can renew it from within Japan, but that requires a trip to your embassy (which may not be located anywhere near where you live) and a transfer of your visa. It's far easier to renew your passport at home in time to get your visa before leaving.
- Scan all of your important documents onto a flash drive for safe keeping. Passport pages, driver's license (bring your original as well), a photo of your degree, etc. You never know when you'll need these things.
- Collect all of your important documents (including bank and tax records) someplace that a family member can access them if needed.
- Get an IDP. International Driving Permits are usable for up to one year from date of entry into Japan.

Even if you don't plan to drive, it can be useful in case of emergency or if you decide you want to drive later. In the US, you can get an IDP from AAA.

- Write down the names, phone numbers, and addresses of your Japanese contacts to carry with you, just in case. This should include someone from your workplace.

- Sign up for a webmail service like Gmail so you can access your email from anywhere.

- Establish an account with an online bank. Being able to access your funds online and send money will make life much easier. When I first moved here, internet banking was a very new thing, but it made paying bills back home (for students loans) very convenient. If you're clever, you can figure out how to use your online bank with PayPal to transfer funds overseas.

- Call your credit providers and tell them that you'll be traveling to Japan for an open period of time. Failure to do so may result in charges being flagged as "suspected fraud" and being denied. This can be major hassle to correct. Hint: due to residency conditions in your credit contract, you probably shouldn't tell them that you are *moving* to Japan.

- You may want to get a new card specifically to use in Japan. It can make tracking your finances easier, and you can also find a card with travel and frequent flier bonuses, which are bound to become very useful. Credit companies often offer special rates and deals for new card accounts, so you can probably save yourself a respectable amount of money if you shop around.

- Get familiar with the metric system. Nobody in Japan has ever heard of pounds or miles. Sorry, Americans.

- Join social networks online. You can use Facebook and other services to find friends in Japan. It'll also make it much easier to communicate with your friends back home.
- Cancel any recurring subscriptions or services. This isn't really a moving checklist, but this is one thing that's easy (and expensive) to forget.
- Study up a bit on basic English grammar. Even if you aren't going to be teaching, you will inevitably be asked English questions. It's always great if you can have a (correct) answer.
- Gather up as much cash as you can. Whether you choose to exchange it to yen before or after arrival in Japan is up to you. The prices in major cities are pretty even. You may want to purchase traveler's cheques in yen. Either way, remember that cash is the easiest currency to spend.
- Get in shape. Travel can take its toll on your health, and you may not have access to a gym for your first few weeks in Japan. Try to be as healthy as possible when you arrive. It really will make your life much easier.

WHAT TO BRING WITH, WHAT TO LEAVE BEHIND

Moving abroad can be stressful. There are a million questions. A lot of those are about what to bring with you and what to leave behind. Here is a guide to some of the most common concerns.

Bring With

- **Prescription medicine** - Bring your prescription and any drugs in their original packaging. Japan thinks drugs are evil, so their laws are very strict.
- **Laptop computer** - convenient and useful. Enough said.
- **A suit** - you will almost certainly need formal dress at some point in your stay, no matter where you end up working.
- **Birth control pills** - I hear that you can get these in Japan now, but they may not be offered in the dosage and type you're used to, and some doctors apparently refuse to prescribe them. To be on the safe side, bring them with you.
- **Vitamins** - For those health conscious among us, vitamin supplements are a necessity, and the ones available in Japan are generally low potency and low quality. Bring a supply with you.
- **Photos** - For your own use and to show curious coworkers or students.
- **Power transformer** - If you are from North America, most of your gadgets will run on Japan's 100V current (though sensitive devices will probably require a transformer). Those from other areas of the

world will probably need an adapter of some sort. Or you could just buy all your electronics here.

Leave Behind

- **Recreational drugs** - Seriously, I should not have to include this point, but please be aware that ALL drugs are taken much more seriously in Japan than where you live now. You *will* be **arrested and deported** if you are caught with recreational drugs in *any* quantity.
- **Extra shoes** - in the past, it was difficult to find shoes in large sizes, but they are much more widely available now. Shoes are heavy and difficult to carry. Unless you have very large feet, a couple of pairs is all you'll need.
- **"Indoor" shoes** - people freak out about having the right indoor shoes (especially those who will be ALTs). Don't worry about it. Every place you go will have slippers, and you can buy shoes here once you know what you need.
- **Condoms** - Japanese brands now offer larger sizes, but they still feel different from what you're used to. American condoms are available from amazon.jp and other places.
- **CDs, DVDs, etc.** - Get an iPod for your music and rip any DVDs onto a portable hard disc. The DVDs will not play on Japanese machines (unless they are special "region free" players).
- **Gifts for coworkers** - You are not Japanese. As such, you are not expected to behave as a Japanese person does. Nobody will think poorly of you if you don't manage to fit gifts into your suitcase with all of your worldly possessions as you move your entire life across an ocean. Nobody really wants a box of

crushed cookies anyway. Leave the souvenirs and instead impress them with your personality and willingness to learn.

- **Books** - If you really love reading, I suggest looking into Amazon's Kindle. Books are heavy and expensive to ship. Only carry them if they're extremely important to you.

- **Pets** - I know Fluffy is your best friend, soul mate, child, whatever, but bringing him to Japan with you is a major pain for both of you. If everything doesn't work out just right, you could be responsible for a very long and expensive quarantine. Arrange for your pets to have a good home before planning to move to Japan.

- **Too many clothes** - There are stores in Japan, and though it isn't always cheap, you can find good deals on winter coats and such if you shop around. Carrying or shipping heavy clothes takes plenty of time and money too, so you may as well just pack light and plan to use some cash once you're here.

FIRST STEPS ON ARRIVAL

The first things you have to do upon arrival in Japan will vary depending on your location and contract. JETs will just have to remain conscious and do as they are told. Some companies may meet you at the airport. Others may give you directions for making your way to an orientation somewhere. Some may give you very little to go on.

In any event, there are a few things you'll need to do promptly. Besides the obvious, such as finding a place to live (which your employer will probably help you with), there are a couple you may not have thought of. There's a good chance your employer will remind you of your obligations and give you some advice for fulfilling them. What follows is a summary of a couple of the really important items.

Gaijin Card

I'll discuss this in more detail later, but suffice it to say that registering for your Alien Registration Card (often referred to by foreign residents as the "Gaijin Card") is a top priority. This is going to be necessary for you to do almost anything else in Japan. Apply for it first at your local municipal office and get the note that shows that you've applied. It will take a few weeks to get the actual card, but the note they give you can be used in its place for a few weeks.

Bank Account

Your employer really should help you with this, but in the event that they do not, you'll have to do it on your own. You will very likely be paid by direct transfer into your account. You'll need your passport and Alien Registration (or note of application) to set up an account, and the bank clerk will probably be extremely confused about the process of creating an account for you. Just relax and keep a positive attitude, and you'll make it through all right.

Reentry Permit

Your visa is only good for one entry into Japan from abroad. That means that, if you travel to Korea or visit home, you can be detained at border control or deported when you attempt to come back into the country. The way to get around this is to purchase a "Reentry Permit" from immigration. It'll cost you an afternoon and 6000 yen. Just take your passport to the office, fill out the form, and take a number.

Everything else you need to do urgently is really common sense. Things like getting a mobile phone will be a matter of personal preference and accommodation is specific to contract and situation. If you take care of the three items above, you shouldn't have official trouble with whatever other choices you make.

YOUR GAIJIN CARD

"Gaijin Card" is what most of the non-Japanese I know in Japan call their Alien Registration Cards.

The Alien Registration Card is easy enough to obtain. Simply report to the nearest town hall or city office with your passport and a couple of passport-sized photos, fill out an application, and pay a small fee. You'll receive a note with your name on it that tells interested parties that you have registered legally (and you can use this card to open a bank account, among other things).

After a couple of weeks to a month or so, you should get a post card in the mail informing you that your card is ready. Return to the city office with that card and the note they gave you when you applied, and exchange them for your shiny new Gaijin Card.

A rundown of the information it includes:
- Photo
- Full name
- Nationality
- Date of birth
- Place of birth
- Passport number
- Date of entry into Japan
- Address in Japan
- Visa status
- Visa expiration date
- Vocation
- Employer's name and address

If any of this information changes, you must go to the municipal office and make corrections within 30 days.

To many foreign residents, that seems like an awful lot of very personal information to be required to carry at all times. You will be required to present this card for any number of services you wish to receive, including opening a bank account, getting a mobile phone, and other situations in which the necessity of the clerk having access to your passport number is questionable.

The only time you can be forced to show your ARC is if the police decide to charge you with a crime. The law states that you do not have to show the card to police if you do not want to, but this is probably not the best strategy for staying out of trouble if your Japanese isn't excellent and you aren't totally certain that you haven't broken any laws (and I mean *any*).

Similarly, businesses are allowed to deny service to anyone who doesn't provide the information they decide to require. Some businesses have a distrust of non-Japanese, and are apparently legally entitled to have policies that discriminate on the basis of national origin (even though this violates UN regulations, the Japanese government seems to feel that it's OK). In such cases, you can argue about it and get angry, or you can simply show the card and fill out whatever forms you are asked for.

I'm not going to get into the politics of the Gaijin Card. The important thing to remember is that it's illegal not to carry it with you at all times while you live in Japan. You can be arrested or deported for not having it with you - even "by accident." If you are very lucky in court and apologize profusely for betraying of the trust of your Japanese hosts, you may get off with a fine.

The simple fact is that you must register as a resident alien, and you must carry your ARC with you. This is really important, so please, please just have it with you at all times in Japan.

WORKING FOR A JAPANESE COMPANY

If you are considering a move to Japan to work, there are a few things you'll need to know about the typical Japanese work environment.

Bare in mind that, in JET lingo, every situation is different. Every office and industry has different standards. Every supervisor has different expectations. Every contract is going to stipulate different conditions and responsibilities and compensation. Still, there are a few things you can almost count on, and knowing the differences between how work gets done in Japan and where you're from can be a big advantage.

Here are a few things you can count on:

Work Hours

Japanese workers take pride in working too much. For example, schoolteachers often arrive before 7am to coach sports, teach all day, have a few meetings with other teachers, supervise club activities, then spend a couple of hours grading papers and planning lessons until 8pm. If there is a sports meet on Saturday, they will have to get up early for that (and they happen quite often). This is not an unusual schedule for a junior high teacher.

In most offices too, very few people will be seen packing up and leaving when 5pm rolls around. Staying late shows dedication to the job.

Regardless of where you work, you'll find that your Japanese coworkers will always tend to work late. You don't have to do this. If your contract stipulates certain working hours, there is no reason you need to work outside those hours unless you have tasks that require doing do.

Sick Days

On a related note, you may notice that Japanese people don't like to take sick days. In fact, many will use vacation days instead of sick days. I can only imagine that this is a way of apologizing to the employer for having the audacity to get sick and put a burden on everyone else. More often, you'll see your coworkers show up to the office despite illness (often wearing surgical masks).

In this case too, I suggest staying home if you are sick and taking paid leave to do so. You have nothing to gain by mimicking the false sense of obligation many Japanese workers have for their employers.

Bonuses

Japanese salaries can seem quite low on first glance, but most Japanese companies pay their employees two major bonuses each year - one in summer and one in winter. These bonuses are often around two to three times the usual monthly salary, so they are a major source of income.

Most non-Japanese workers do not get bonuses. This is a contractual issue that varies for each position, but as a rule, you will not be getting any bonus that isn't precisely spelled out. If you have Japanese coworkers, they will assume that you do get a bonus. At one school I worked at, a coworker found out my monthly salary from the board of education (great privacy, right?) and was angry to find out that I made as much money as he did (he had been teaching for many years and always worked late, while I left each day at 4). Of course, including bonuses, he made roughly 50% more than I did each year, but I had a hard time explaining that to him.

Chain of Command

It works like this: First, you discuss any issues amongst your coworkers - beginning with the person who sits closest to you (even if it happens to be the tea lady) and then the members of your team. Then one of you will approach the immediate supervisor. You'll have to explain the whole situation, and he will then ask for input from the people who sit near him and then the relevant people involved in the issue. He may look up some of the rules or call someone and ask them to look up the rules. Then he'll consider the options. If, unfortunately, there is a decision that cannot be voided by following a predetermined rule, the supervisor will have to consult his boss. All the while, you are waiting.

The problem is that nobody in any government or business actually has any authority. They have tasks and roles, but not the power to make decisions. Deciding is always done by committee and the results are preserved as rules and procedures to follow in similar cases in the future.

The chain of command is important. It gives clear roles to everyone involved so they don't have to be confused about what to do or worry about thinking. It also removes any unfortunate situations involving accountability for errors or negligence (and convenient "forgetting" happens all too often in some offices).

There is always at least one figurehead who signs things and attends meetings. Then there is the supervisor who sees to it that the work gets done. There will be someone who takes care of administrative tasks. There is usually someone who makes tea and handles mail and cleaning and various simple tasks. There are also teams for certain tasks or areas, and each one has a leader. Some people are on several teams.

If anything needs to get done, it has to go through the chain of command. You need to know who is in your team and who is the leader. Know who your supervisor is. Being a foreigner, you can often get away with breaking the chain and approaching supervisors directly on important issues, but don't abuse this because it makes your team members feel small. After all, they need something to do.

Every office or workplace has a different chain of command and a different level of formality. Pay attention to figure this out as soon as you can, because it will make getting things done much easier once you know whom to talk to and whom not to bother.

Efficiency

This is one place where you can forget any image you may have of Japan as a technological leader. Though Japan is obsessed with technology (they have computer controlled toilet seats) in many respects, it simply does not show at the typical office. Most record keeping is still done manually and on paper. Forms are stamped, hole-punched, and placed in binders which are stored in cabinets locked with keys hung on the wall on the other side of the room.

Computers are widely used, but not well. Most machines are several years old and run old versions of common software. Only in technical or design fields would you expect to see new computers with up-to-date programs. Nobody in your office will have administrative network access, so you will have to ask the designated person if you want to remove the icons of useless apps from your desktop. This person will then have to ask your supervisor if it's all right, but your supervisor won't understand what the issue is. When Japanese people don't understand something, they usually just say no (better safe than sorry...).

OK, so I'm generalizing and maybe even exaggerating (but really only a little), but you get the idea. Japanese offices are run on systems that are at least 50 years old. This is so because the people who run the offices are old, and they learned their management techniques from people who are even older.

Part of the problem goes back to chain of command issues. Reorganizing and bringing things up to date may have a positive impact on efficiency in the long run, but it isn't easy to make the transition. The people who would have to approve such changes are not at all confident in their abilities to learn new things.

Inefficiency in Japan's Employment Solution and Culture
Imagine for a minute what would happen if a Japanese city office updated their systems, computerized their records, and began using technology to improve workflow. Things could get done in less time and with less error. Sounds good at first, but all this increased speed and performance means that fewer people would be able to get the same amount of work done. And that means fewer jobs.

In Japan, even very small towns have a large public office. The town I lived in as a JET had fewer than 5,000 residents, but we had a town hall, three schools, two kindergartens, a sports facility, a senior center, a library and community center, and a small museum that employed several hundred of those residents. The money for all these facilities came in the form of subsidies from the national government to make sure that there would be enough employers in the town for everyone to have a job. (This kind of wastefulness is widespread in Japan and one of the reasons that the country never recovered from recession in the late 90s.)

Without all that, our town was really just a farming community growing *negi* and *konnyaku*. If operations were streamlined at the town hall, maybe 100 people could lose their jobs. In such a small town, that's a big number.

But it's not just the jobs at stake. It's the whole culture of employment. If things were easier, working hours would be shorter. It would no longer be necessary to show up for work on Saturday morning. People would have more energy and time to spend with their families and friends. In short, the entire underpinning of Japanese society would unravel.

You'll often hear the word *ganbatte* or *ganbare* in Japan. Roughly translated, it means to try hard. In Japan, *ganbare* is much more important than performance in almost everything. It does not matter to most of your coworkers if you don't know how to do your job. If you show up early and stay late everyday, they will praise your spirit and think highly of you. If you're coming up for a promotion, showing up on Saturdays will be a big help, even if you do nothing but shuffle papers from one pile to another and take several coffee breaks.

The appearance of trying hard is of huge importance in Japan. If everything suddenly got a lot easier in the office, that appearance would be shattered, and the workers wouldn't know what to do with themselves. There would be no more beer and ramen after late nights at the office. There would be no more gulping down energy drinks on the train in the morning. Japan would look much different from the way it does now.

I seriously believe that Japanese society cannot stand up to efficiency. Inefficiency is built in to every gathering or group at the most fundamental levels - especially in work culture. You will see it on a daily basis if you live here. It can be extremely frustrating to accomplish seemingly simple tasks in such environments, so be prepared to deal with it because, no matter how many great improvements you suggest in your office, chances are that your coworkers are secretly afraid of making changes that could make anyone look bad and/or take away their *ganbare*.

Nomikai

Nomikai, enkai, and various other *-kai* are parties, and they are an important part of the working culture in Japan. These office-sanctioned drunk-fests can be a lot of fun, depending on your personality. They can be a great way to get to know your coworkers outside of the office and find out things you don't feel comfortable asking at work.

Japanese people live in a pretty repressed culture, especially at work, where they are governed by endless rules, obligations, and the expectations of others. These periodic parties are a way to let off steam and build trust and positive relations among coworkers, and they're very important for those reasons.

However, I've heard some people complain that the drunken behavior of their Japanese coworkers is inappropriate and offensive at times. Indeed, drunkenness lowers our inhibitions, and most Japanese are extremely inhibited under normal conditions. Given the chance to take off their professional masks, many Japanese exhibit the kind of behavior you may expect at a frat party. Any latent sexism is likely to come to the surface. Insensitive remarks about your cultural origins may be spoken without thinking. If this kind of thing bothers you, you should probably not go to the parties.

You should know that these are usually celebratory events. Nobody is attempting to make you feel unwelcome or offend you. Japanese people on the whole still do not know how to deal with people from other cultures, and drinking manners vary widely by country. If you can roll with it, just try to have a good time without taking offense. Chances are, you'll really enjoy hanging with your coworkers in a relaxed atmosphere.

One last thing to remember about *nomikai* is that, the next day, it will be as if it never happened. Tanaka-san will not comment on your lovely drunken duet of "We are the World." It's over and gone, and there is work to be done. The girl from the next office who laughed at all your jokes on Friday evening probably does not want you to ask her out on Monday afternoon.

Even when you play with coworkers, you have to remember that work and play are sharply divided in most Japanese workplaces. This may seem like a strange way to act about something that is meant to improve morale, but it's also a way to avoid embarrassment.

Of course, there's plenty more where these points came from. Books have been written about Japan's work culture, and I recommend reading a couple of them if you plan to work in a Japanese office (though be sure to remember that they may be exaggerated or out-of-date). Still the above points are a good starting place for attempting to make sense of the Japanese work place and fit with your coworkers.

Tips from a Recruiter

What follows on the next few pages is an interview I conducted via email with a friend of mine who works for one of the larger companies hiring foreigners to teach English in Japan.

He still interviews hundreds of candidates each year. In fact, if you apply for a teaching job through a dispatch company, there's a possibility that you'll meet him. Since that could be unfair, he asked me not to identify him in this report. As a result, some of the answers are purposefully vague, but I think you'll learn a lot by reading between the lines about the kinds of things real recruiters are looking at in interviews.

This is a peak into the mind and thought process of the people who read your cover letter, check your resume, follow up on your references, and ultimately decide whether or not to offer you a contract. You should definitely refer back to this interview (and re-read the recruiting materials) before clicking "send" or "submit" on any application for a teaching job. Doing so will help you get an image of the people to whom you are actually addressing your communication.

Following the interview, I've assembled a list of a few tips specifically for interviewing in Japan.

The Interview

Roughly how many people do you hire? How many do you not hire?

I hire throughout the year, but could hire anywhere from 50 to 100 teachers for April as that is the biggest recruiting time for teachers in public school.

It depends on how big your company is. People who would drop out, we would have to replace so about 10 a year, and then for

September starts we would do another 50 - 100. We worked with another office and helped them recruit as well.

In percentage wise, considering that the salary was not the highest in the industry, we basically hired about 80 % of our applicants. Mind you, we were more strict in screening the resumes because if they didn't have what we were looking for, there was no point to interview them.

Among qualified candidates, what was the biggest difference between those who "got in" and those who didn't?

Japanese level, amount of experience as a teacher in japan, and personality. Also, people that are late for an interview are a definite no-no in my books. Also, if they lied on their resume about their experience, or they had bad references.

Usually you can tell whether the applicant is good for the position within the first 2 minutes of meeting them. If they are confident and not cocky, and presentable and are genuinely interested in the job, we would generally be interested in them.

What about people with little or no experience?

We did have a few people that slipped through the cracks. They may have been friends with our current teachers, had good Japanese skills, or had a lot of experience with children. A genuine interest and enthusiasm and the willingness to learn about Japan and the culture was also a top point. Being organized and prepared for the interview.

Generally though, if one hadn't taught before, the level of Japanese was a huge plus (this is for public schools).

What's the biggest mistake people make when applying or interviewing for a job in Japan?

Spelling errors on their resume, not knowing what the job entails, bringing their spouse or partner to the interview, not wearing proper interview clothing, walking in and saying that you need sponsorship. (If the company really likes you, then they may be able to sponsor you but they do have to jump through hoops. It is also about timing. If the company gets a visa for you, but you do not get it back in time before the start of work, then they will not consider you for the job).

What advice would you give somebody who wants to move to Japan?

Do your research as to what exactly you want to do, start taking Japanese lessons, start tutoring or volunteering at summer camps with kids. Do not come to Japan hoping you will learn everything once you get there. If it sounds as though you know nothing about Japan, companies will not be interested in you.

What do you look for in a resume, cover letter, or other first contact?

For teaching we look for the following:

Teaching experience in Japan or abroad, tutoring experience, experience with working with children, travel experience, Japanese language skills, well rounded individual. Someone who can show personality on a cover letter without sounding like a cliche or desperate.

When first meeting them, we are definitely looking for enthusiastic, team players, that can roll with the punches. If you want to take control and seem too strong, this type of personality often does not mesh with Japanese people well.

We also look for someone who can take direction well and is genuinely interested in Japan and teaching.

How should candidates prepare for an interview?

Research the company, research the type of job that they are doing, if you don't know anything about the job, to look at forums and find out what it is about, have questions, have all the documents that we have requested you to bring, an ironed business attire outfit, and definitely not be late. It is also nice to have reference letters with you.

What should people look for in a company?

Don't ask about the salary during the interview. It is tacky and makes the company think that you are just looking at money.

Things you should look for in a company:

Does this type of company suit you when it comes to your needs? Are they able to sponsor your visa, give you support throughout the year, if they give reviews of your work performance, if there are ways to advance in the company, what the turnover rate has been for the company (*this can often be a good sign as to what the company may be like), if there are rewards or bonuses given, what if any benefits a company has, if they provide assistance in daily Japanese life.

Any other advice?

The English teaching industry can be small. Never burn your bridges with any company. Every experience can be learned upon.

Thank you.

Some Unconventional Advice

General Tips:

- Dress nicely, but not too nicely. Everyone knows that you need to dress nicely for an interview, but don't forget why you're here - to show what sets you apart from other candidates with similar experience. You also have to be comfortable. I interviewed for JET wearing a light sweater over a t-shirt and made it on the shortlist. If wearing a tie with a stiff collar prevents you form engaging with your interviewers, you are going to have a tough time making a good impression.
- Despite the focus on appearance, remember that who you are matters more than how you look. The whole purpose of the interview is to ask you enough questions that the company can get an idea about how you will represent them. Be competent. Be classy. Being pretty is just a bonus.
- Clean your shoes. Don't wear sneakers. Your shoes don't need to be stylish, but they do need to be appropriate and clean. If you interview at a Japanese office, you may be asked to remove your shoes at the door, and this calls attention to your footwear. Cleanliness matters.
- When sitting at a table, it's best to keep your hands in your lap. Otherwise they can become a distraction.
- When sitting in a chair with no table, it's OK to cross your legs. Make sure to cross at the knee.
- You may be handed business cards. I hesitate to even mention it here because some people overemphasize its importance, but you should know the "proper" way to accept cards. Take the card with both hands and actually look at it. It's a good idea to repeat the person's name as you read it, so you can remember it later. Do not just shove the card in your pocket. You

can set it on the table during your interview and slide it into a shirt or jacket pocket when you gather yourself to exit. Just remember that the card represents a person, so act as if it is significant and valuable.

- You will likely be offered tea. It's good manners to wait until you are invited to actually drink it, but feel free to sip at your leisure after that. If you don't like it, you can just take a sip and then leave the rest.
- Don't touch your face - it makes you look less trustworthy.
- Don't try to force eye contact. In the West, we think eye contact shows confidence, but in Japan, it is considered invasive.
- If your interviewer is Japanese, use simple buzzwords like "energetic" and "trust." I don't mean to put anyone down, but most Japanese professionals are suckers for English buzzwords. They are easier to remember than more sophisticated language. Keep in mind your audience when you are trying to make a good impression.
- Remember that you are not being hired for you ability to express yourself eloquently in English. You are being hired for your ability to be a team player and communicate with people who have very little English skill. It's best to express yourself simply (but don't take it too far and limit yourself to monosyllabic words either).
- Don't correct an interviewer's English. Japanese use a lot of English words, but they often have different meanings. For example, "fight" means to try hard. Don't dwell on odd phrasing or incorrect wording. Just move on.
- Don't be afraid to make jokes if you feel they are appropriate.

- Ask lots of questions. It's silly to assume you know anything unless you've got a lot of experience. Just ask. If the interviewer doesn't know, or if the answer varies depending on placement (very, very common), don't press them.
- On the other hand, don't guess in order to answer their questions either. Clarify and qualify. The better you understand the question, the better you can give an honest and intelligent answer. You'll impress interviewers more by being open about what you don't know (hence showing that you are willing to learn) than you will be trying to act as if you have all the answers.
- The interviewer may appear to make a lot of assumptions about you. Be cool about this. Correct them about anything that you feel is grossly inaccurate or makes you look bad, but don't go overboard. For example, if an interviewer makes an off-hand remark about Americans eating a lot of meat compared to the Japanese, it's OK to tell them that you're a vegetarian, but don't take that as a launching point for a diatribe against the meat industry. Better to just let it slide. Japanese people (your coworkers, your students, and people in your community) will make a lot of (probably untrue) assumptions about you and your country. You may not like it, but you'll have to deal with it - especially if you're trying to make a good impression during an interview.
- If you eat before the interview, be sure to brush your teeth and wash your hands.
- Smile.
- Say "thank you" as often as you can.

Big-Picture Questions:

We covered some typical questions in the interviewing section of the Guide, but I wanted to add a few more here.

- Why do you want to live in Japan? (Yes, it's obvious, but you *will* be asked, so make sure you have a good answer that shows what a good candidate you are. Hint: don't say "I love Japanese culture," unless you can cite examples besides anime and sushi.)
- Are you married? Do you have a boyfriend / girlfriend? Do you have any children? (If you answer yes, be sure you have some realistic and well-thought-out plans about how living in Japan will affect your situation.)
- How long do you plan to stay in Japan?
- Why do you want to teach?
- What were you like in junior high school (or whatever level of school the interview is for)?
- Tell me about some challenges you expect to face while working in Japan. (Be very careful about the assumptions you make here.)
- Tell me about a time that you learned from a mistake. (Japanese people love to *ganbare*, which means "try hard." Wow them with a story that taught you to "never give up," which is a great catch phrase they love to hear.)

There are, of course, lots of variations on these themes, but just be sure to come prepared with a good backstory and some responses to these kinds of prompts. The interview isn't just about the job - it's about your personality. Expect questions about what kind of person you are.

Stupid Questions:

The following are less common, but it's good to be prepared so you don't get thrown for a loop.

- What would you do if two students began fighting during a class you are supervising?
- Do you like Japanese women / men?
- Do you have a gun? (Guns are illegal in Japan, but Japanese people are under the impression that all Americans carry them. The best option is just to say that you don't own one - even if you do.)
- Can you use chopsticks?
- Can you eat fish?
- What do your parents think about you moving to Japan? (If you have an "untraditional" family, just keep your answer simple here. Let the interviewer know that your folks support your decisions and that you hope they can visit sometime.)
- Do you like alcohol? (You don't want to come off as an alcoholic or a prude here. Drinking parties are an important part of work culture, though it's OK not to drink. Just don't act morally superior about it.)
- What do you think about WW2? (Terrible question. Sometimes gets asked. Just remember that you weren't there, so avoid making too many generalizations. It's best to redirect - talk about how glad you are that Japan is now such a symbol of peace and global cooperation.)
- Japanese students are very shy. How would you try to teach students who don't like to speak out in front of their classmates? (The whole "shy" bit is BS, but you still have to answer this question. The right answer involves encouraging without putting anyone on the spot.)

And you get the idea... Just remember to answer based on what you know, not what you assume. Be sincere. Some interviewers will ask stupid and confrontational questions. Be like the Fonz - be cool. Poise is a better weapon than wit when faced with ignorant questions, so be prepared with answers and redirections that show how diplomatic and friendly you are.

RESOURCES

In this section I have included a list of internet resources to check out for further information on topics related to moving to and working in Japan.

Some of these links lead to Japanese pages. Look for links in English on the site.

Japan Information

National Tourism Organization - www.jnto.go.jp
Official information resource for tourists

Japan Guide - www.japan-guide.com
My mother loves this site for finding information about various places in Japan. I usually check it out when I'm planning on traveling.

Web Japan - www.web-japan.org
Nice site with lots Japan-related content and a killer links section.

Job Boards

Gaijin Pot - www.gaijinpot.com
Probably the biggest and most popular board. Easy to use, but lots of competition.

Ohayo Sensei - www.ohayosensei.com
Great resource. Only updated twice a month, but includes some excellent jobs. Email them for the current issue.

Daijob - www.daijob.com/en/
Jobs in a wide variety of fields, but most of them require some Japanese ability.

JALT Listing - www.jalt-publications.org/tlt/jobs/
Lists private school and university jobs.

Jobs in Japan - www.jobsinjapan.com
Some opportunities that aren't on other Job boards. You'll have to make contact via email.

Career Cross Japan - www.careercross.com
Career Cross Japan includes many listings for jobs other than teaching. It has great search functions, but most positions require Japanese skills.

There are other job boards out there, but these are the biggest and most up-to-date.

Regional Information and Classifieds

Hokkaido Insider - www.ne.jp/asahi/hokkaido/kenhartmann/index.html
Information (some free, some paid) on jobs in Hokkaido

Kansai Flea Market - www.kfm.to
A print and online magazine that offers a great classified section with tons of job listings in and around Osaka, Kyoto, and Kobe.

Fukuoka Now - www.fukuoka-now.com
Online magazine and classifieds for Fukuoka area

Get Hiroshima - www.gethiroshima.com
Online information site for Hiroshima area

JET Programme Links

Official Site - www.jetprogramme.org
Background and application information

Big Daikon - www.bigdaikon.com
Opinions and experiences of those on JET. Remember, most people (myself included) loved JET, but others don't get as much

out of it. Read BD for perspective, but don't let it discourage you.

Eikaiwa

AEON - www.aeonet.com

Berlitz - www.berlitz.com

ECC - www.japanbound.com

GEOS - www.geoscareer.com

James English School - www.jesjapan.com

Dispatch Companies

Altia Central - www.altia-jp.com
Altia is a company that I've worked for. They have good training and fair contracts.

Interac - www.interacnetwork.com
Interac is arguably the largest dispatch company placing thousand of ALTs throughout Japan each year. Also check out the Japanese site at www.interac.co.jp

Westgate Corporation - www.westgate.co.jp
Dispatch to universities in in the Tokyo area

International Staffing Services - www.iss.edu
Staffing for international private schools

Services for Meeting Private Students

ABC kara - www.abckara.com
Teacher/student matching company with good service and fair rates

7act - www.7act.net
Highest rated private tutoring service for client satisfaction

Volunteer Opportunities

WWOOF Japan - www.wwoofjapan.com
Work on organic farms and other out-of-the-way places to experience a different side of Japan

United Planet - www.unitedplanet.org
Volunteer opportunities in Japan include working with Non Profit Organizations which provide services for the local community.

Service Civil International - www.sci-ivs.org
SCI is an exchange organization that sends volunteers on 2-3 week international work projects and long term 3-12 month opportunities in over 50 countries, including Japan. The $250 application fee covers lodging, meals, and minimal health insurance.

Recommended Forums

ESL Cafe - www.eslcafe.com
Probably the oldest site of its kind. The international job forums are huge and full of useful insight, old information, helpful old timers, and pissed off ex-employees. In other words, there's a lot of good info, but you shouldn't believe everything you read there.

Your Rights

David Aldwinckle - www.debito.org
A naturalized Japanese citizen and activist with lots of information about working at Japanese universities, your rights as a foreign resident, and some funny stories.

General Union - www.generalunion.org
Information on the Japanese labor laws (which *do* apply to foreign workers)

Visas and Immigration

Ministry of Foreign Affairs Japan - www.mofa.go.jp
Official visa and immigration information

Driving Information

Japan Auto Federation - www.jaf.or.jp
The easiest place to get license translations and the Rules of the Road brochure. Also specific details about the process for obtaining a Japanese license. As laws change, JAF info will always be up to date.

Learning Japanese

All Japanese All the Time - www.alljapaneseallthetime.com
Extreme program to get fluent fast

JLPT Study Page - www.jlptstudy.com
Indexed study guide to all levels of the Japanese Language Proficiency Test

Nihongo Resources - www.nihongoresources.com
Guide to Japanese language, including dialects

Services for Living in Japan

GoLloyd's - www.lloydstsb.co.jp
A service for reliable and speedy transfer of funds from your Japanese bank account to a foreign account. Costs 2000 yen per transfer, but is only takes a day to process.

World Link - www.worldlink-tel.com
Discount service for international calling if you use a landline.

Skype - www.skype.com
But why would you use a phone for international calls when you can use Skype from your computer?

Insurance

National Health Insurance - www.kokuho.or.jp
Know what you need to legally reside in Japan

Teaching Resources

Using English - www.usingenglish.com

Boggles World ESL - www.bogglesworldesl.com

Team Taught Pizza - www.ttp.ajet.net

Dave's ESL Café - www.daveseslcafe.com

Genki English - www.genkienglish.net

Cheap Accommodation

J-hoppers - www.j-hoppers.com
Great hostels in several cities with English-speaking staff and good atmosphere

International Tourist Center of Japan - www.itcj.or.jp
This site is maintained by the International Tourist Center of Japan and features an impressive list of lodgings in all price ranges and all regions of Japan.

Japan Youth Hostels - www.jyh.or.jp
This web site is dedicated exclusively to youth hostels in Japan. It is well organized by region and city and features hundreds of low-cost lodging options.

Other Useful Sites

Amazon Japan - www.amazon.jp
Sells almost everything...

Hyperdia - www.hyerdia.com
Information on train schedules for getting around in Japan

OUTRODUCTION

No document can give you *all* the information you need to find employment and prepare to move to another country. However, the principles that underly the specific advice presented here will take you very far towards achieving your goal to live in Japan.

There is a lot about living in Japan that this guide doesn't cover. Information on mobile phone providers, how to get internet service and set up digital cable, using public transport, making insurance claims, etc... But my best advice on these things is the JET mantra: *every situation is different* - ESID.

Not everyone who reads this guide will choose to live in the same areas of the country, and their options will be different. Most people who opt for urban environments won't need to get a driver's license, and Tokyo subway maps will be quite useless to anyone who lives in Osaka. Besides that, I can't tell you how to live your life - what brand of rice to buy or which real estate agent to use. These are personal choices that we all have to make for ourselves based on the information we have available at the time and our own preferences.

There will no doubt be questions you have that aren't addressed in this guide, but more often than not, the best answers will be apparent with a small amount of additional research. The Resources section is included to fill in any gaps, but remember to filter that information through what you've learned here.

Live Your Own Dream

Beyond information, you simply have to go out there and make it happen. There's no adventure in following step-by-step instructions to living someone else's life. If you really wanted that, you probably wouldn't be thinking about moving to another country to begin with.

Now you know pretty much everything you need to know about finding work in Japan - as far as knowledge will take you, anyway. The most important things, you'll have to learn as you go. Through experience.

My Japan experience has taught me more about my own country, and about myself, than I ever thought it would. When you return home after living here, *if* you return home, you'll find that you see things through different eyes than before. And that's the real benefit of living here, the thing that makes it more priceless than anything you'll see on a Master Card commercial.

I wish you the best of luck in your job search and in the other searches that make life interesting.

- Andy